Five potential
Napster moments

Maria's new role — A bridge between insurance and innovation

This is the section where I am going to discuss how to make all our talk about revolutionary innovation a reality.

At Maddock Douglas, part of my job is to imagine products and services in the insurance and financial advice/product space that don't exist yet, but could.

Some would argue that the things I am going to discuss can't happen. Some don't even argue; they just give me that "look" that says, *"you realize you're crazy, right?"*

My husband, Jim, who has spent years in the insurance industry, gave me that look when I shared some of these ideas with him. However, Jim, like me and some of my other insurance friends, has learned a lot from the innovation techniques used by Maddock Douglas. (The ideas that I have discussed so far.) And I am bringing them around, thanks to one of my favorite ideation techniques that we are going to use here.

It revolves around a game called "What Would _____ Do?" The blank varies. Sometimes we will ask ourselves — or our clients — what would a person such as Steve Jobs, Richard Branson or Mark Zuckerberg do? Sometimes we fill in the blank with a company like Amazon, Google or Netflix.

Some call this parallel engineering; some call it stealing; I call it inspiration. Choose your label, but remember that roll-on deodorant was inspired by the ball point pen and Velcro® by the burr.

No matter what you call it, our next step is to figure out how they would solve for the tension in an insight we have spotted. (See Chapter 15.)

Flirting With
The Uninterested

Flirting With
The Uninterested

Innovating in a "Sold, Not Bought" Category

by
Maria Ferrante-Schepis (The Insurance "I")
and
G. Michael Maddock (The Innovation "I")

Advantage®

Published by Advantage, Charleston, South Carolina.
Member of Advantage Media Group.

ADVANTAGE is a registered trademark and the Advantage colophon is a trademark of Advantage Media Group, Inc.

Printed in the United States of America.

ISBN: 978-159932-369-5
LCCN: 2012949829

This publication is designed to provide accurate and authoritative information in regard to the subject matter covered. It is sold with the understanding that the publisher is not engaged in rendering legal, accounting, or other professional services. If legal advice or other expert assistance is required, the services of a competent professional person should be sought.

Advantage Media Group is proud to be a part of the Tree Neutral® program. Tree Neutral offsets the number of trees consumed in the production and printing of this book by taking proactive steps such as planting trees in direct proportion to the number of trees used to print books. To learn more about Tree Neutral, please visit **www.treeneutral.com**. To learn more about Advantage's commitment to being a responsible steward of the environment, please visit **www.advantagefamily.com/green**

Advantage Media Group is a leading publisher of business, motivation, and self-help authors. Do you have a manuscript or book idea that you would like to have considered for publication? Please visit **www.advantagefamily.com** or call **1.866.775.1696**

This book is dedicated to visionary insurance professionals who have proudly contributed to the industry's past successes while remaining committed to inventing its future.

Acknowledgments

We would like to thank all of the people who contributed their talent, hard work and their big brains to make this book better: Paul B. Brown, McRae Williams, Meghan Russell, Nikki Pavey, Deanne DiVito, Terri Hughes, Tim Walker, Noel Childs, Phil Inglis, Cal Engel, Art Karoubas, Kristin Whitehurst, Paul Grachan, Matt Lashey, Cindy Malone, Wes Douglas, Luisa Uriarte, Brett Miller, Doug Stone, Stephanie Savage, Raphael Louis Vitón and Joe Wilds.

The fingerprints of the Maddock Douglas community are all over this book. Our friends and partners are always willing to generously contribute toward our purpose of inspiring and empowering curiosity. Special thanks to Frank EE Grubbich, Paul Umbach, Jacqueline Jones, the Nashville music community, Christi Daughenbaugh, Biro Creative and LearnVest for helping us to envision specific Napster moments.

Finally, we could not have completed this book without the love and support from our spouses and families. Thanks to Jim, Ruth, our kids and our parents for the smiles, the hugs and for being who you are.

We also thank God for all of the above. ☺

Table of Contents

Flip this book over.

Foreword

Whenever I read something by Maria Ferrante-Schepis, one word quickly comes to mind: "Provocative." She always makes you think. Maria has a real knack for making insurance professionals look at the business — and its challenges — in a different light.

Her entrepreneurial writing partner, Mike Maddock, makes a habit out of tackling the toughest industry challenges with unexpected and market-shifting ideas.

In *Flirting With The Uninterested*, Maria and Mike provide an ample supply of new perspective and new ideas.

Life insurance is an industry that desperately needs a wakeup call; innovation has not been its strong point. It has been a slow adapter to new technology, and has done a dismal job of reaching the vast majority of American consumers — the middle market — which is most in need of life insurance protection.

Maria and Mike recognize the industry's shortcomings in reaching today's consumers and call the industry out in no uncertain terms (suggesting what needs to change and how to improve things in the process). I believe, as do the authors, that becoming relevant to the next big customer base — Gen Y — needs to be a key objective of the life insurance industry, and we're a long way from being relevant to this demographic at the moment.

Maria was the first industry thought leader who made me think that the life insurance industry could be "Napstered" by a force currently outside of the industry. If you don't meet the needs and expectations of younger, middle-market consumers who have grown up online, what's to stop another industry from swooping in and reinventing the life insurance market with an effective way to engage the next generation of customers? Maria knows the industry doesn't have to fall victim to outside forces as the music, legal and countless other industries have. And it won't, if life

insurance leaders dump the status quo and start innovating to make life insurance truly relevant to middle-market consumers.

I find the "Napster Moment" section of the book to be particularly fascinating as it helps me envision how widely varying business models could potentially be put to work in the life insurance industry. Asking readers to imagine that our industry was being invented today and did not exist before – and how they would do things – is a textbook example of how Mike and Maria are able to foster innovative thought leadership.

The takeaway: If someone's going to reinvent our industry, why can't it be us?

You will often hear Maria and Mike say, "You can't read the label when you are sitting inside the jar." This book offers "outside-the-jar" insights about how to get the consumer emotionally engaged with life insurance products and drives home that the industry needs to be open to the idea that the engagement and emotion of the product can and should be improved.

Flirting With The Uninterested provides a concise, thoughtful and eye-opening look at the serious problems facing the life insurance industry and walks leaders through the thought processes that can lead to effective responses to those problems. It achieves the goal of inspiring thought and action on the part of anyone interested in guiding the life insurance industry back to being relevant with consumers, who are currently more interested in insuring their stuff than themselves.

Brian Anderson, Editor-in-Chief, *Life Insurance Selling*

Introduction — Moving from the "what" to the "who"

If you can read this, you are too close!

By that I mean that anyone who is interested in *Flirting With The Uninterested* is most likely in a role that deals with the challenge of selling products that are "sold, not bought," and so they may be too close to the problem to see the situation clearly.

You know the difference between bought and not sold categories, of course. People rush out to buy cars, new computers and cell phones. They need to be sold things like insurance coverage in just about all forms. We work in an industry where the conventional wisdom is that no one will ever buy our products unless convinced by someone else to do so.

I spent much of my career in insurance and financial services working within this confine but secretly (and sometimes not so secretly) wishing that it were not true. I believe we'd be better off as an industry, and frankly as a society, if people really wanted to buy what we have to sell. (Additionally, my cocktail party conversations that start with the answer to "What do you do for a living?" might last just a little longer. ☺)

Frustrations are us.

Flirting with the uninterested is literally what insurance industry executives and distributors are doing on a regular basis. The only people clamoring to buy our products are those who are likely the ones we want least. Everyone else couldn't care less.

While what we offer is very logical to the actuarial mind — and potentially others once understood — the average person does not "get it." Yet, most people agree that insurance is important and would not want to be left without it should the need arise. So figuring out how to best create interest among the uninterested is job one.

And to do it we need to think differently. As Einstein said, one should not expect to solve a problem with the same level of intelligence that created it. It is painfully clear that we need a different approach to serving our customers. To date, job one has been confused with making products cheaper and easier to buy, adding more unwieldy guarantees, and copying those products that are already doing well in the market. While there is nothing (much) wrong with those activities, they are not enough to sustain long-term, positive growth as Gen Y — the children of baby boomers who are often referred to as Millennials — emerges as a primary customer.

Additionally, the industry has been complaining for years about the big three problems of commoditization, the shrinking distribution and the growing underserved middle.

Guess what? These aren't the problems. They are the symptoms of a relevance problem that is growing because we simply have done a terrible job understanding the needs of our customers — and future customers — and have been unable to meet them.

It is time we change our industry from a "What" business to a "Who" business.

This book is intended to inspire the creative thought and innovation to do just that. While innovation and insurance in the same sentence may sound like an oxymoron, there are enlightened leaders in a number of companies within our industry rising to the task. They recognize that, in this rapid-paced, competitive environment, we can no longer deliver what we have done in the past to people who are uninterested at best.

If we do not do something to improve the consumers' opinions of our industry, grow our ability to distribute products effectively, serve the underserved, and combat commoditization, we will wake up one day and find that somebody has reinvented the game without us.

And it probably won't be another insurance company. It will more likely be a company you have never thought of as your competition. You won't even see the knockout punch coming.

I don't want that to happen.

Having spent 20-plus years in the executive ranks in insurance companies, I know the kind of change I will be advocating in the pages ahead is not easy. Insurance company cultures are averse to risk, despite being in the risk business. Silos and corporate bureaucracy reward status quo and punish failure. And failure — fast and forward — is a key to successful innovation. However, even though it is hard, it does not give us an excuse to put it aside — or give up. We have no choice. Someone has to innovate. I am hoping it will be you.

If you are deeply committed to the insurance industry, I challenge you to read this book. I promise it will arm you for the battle ahead and show you how to use innovation as the ultimate weapon to save the industry we both love.

Best,
Maria

In 1990, Tom Cain, a mentor and feisty old ad man from Chicago, payed me a backhanded compliment. He said, "Michael, you know how I know you are going to be successful? Because you are too G**Damn stupid to realize you shouldn't be doing what you are doing!"

It turns out he was right. Being naive—intentionally or not—is the secret sauce of the most innovative leaders. As a young, inexperienced professional, I was naturally naive. As I grew older, I had to learn how to stay that way.

Marshall McLuhan had it right when he said, "I don't know who discovered water, but I am pretty sure it wasn't a fish." The hard-earned expertise that you have won't always help you see where you need to go, even when the answer is right in front of you.

Occasionally, an enlightened leader decides that it is time to objectively hear from the customer. He decides it is time to transform from being a "What we sell" company to a "Who we sell to" company. That's what this book is about. That's what the insurance industry needs. That's what we are going to help you do.

Mike

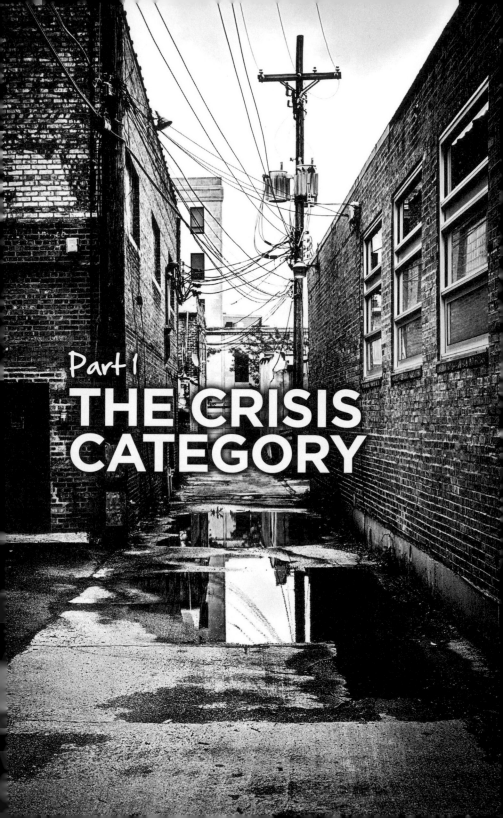

Part 1

THE CRISIS
CATEGORY

CHAPTER 1

The product isn't the problem: They are just not that into you

The problem is you — not them.

The fact that people are not lining up for what you have to sell is not because they are "dumb," or "they don't understand how important our products are," or "they just don't get it."

The problem is YOU. You have not explained simply, clearly and in words THEY use every day why they desperately need what you have.

You can do it.

How?

First, by understanding the new consumer better.

Then (and only then), by innovating. By creating what's new, what's next. More specifically, by making customer involvement and emotion part of everything you do.

But before I even begin to talk about that, you need to truly understand why you need to change how you are currently doing business. I will talk about that here and then introduce some of the basic tenets of innovating effectively — and explain why it is so important to know what business we are really in. (Hint: The answer may surprise you.)

Bill Murray is a great innovator — or at least he played one in the movies. In the 1984 film *Ghostbusters*, Murray's character, Dr. Peter Venkman, and his cohorts spend a long time inventing a revolutionary new technology to get rid of the pesky apparitions that are gradually taking over New York City. But what is strange (or even stranger) about that story is that the people of New York didn't embrace the new technology right away. The amount of ghosts ripe for the busting had to hit a critical mass before the alarm bells started to ring. Before that point,

Murray and his colleagues sat around like a bunch of lonely Maytag® repairmen, with only a petty cash drawer's worth of lo mein to live on.

What lesson can we learn from this? Well, it seems clear that innovation takes time, foresight, patience and a strong constitution *(and perhaps a good sense of humor)*.

Over a decade ago—when people still put film in cameras—our company was working with Kodak. At the time, there were other companies getting into the film business. When asked about the new competitors, the most senior R&D leader from Kodak assured us they were not competitors at all. Kodak's film, paper and chemicals were so superior, he said, that he did not see them as a threat. He was correct—sort of. Kodak had spent decades perfecting accurate imaging, and they were the undisputed leader in quality.

Unfortunately for Kodak, Fuji had entered the market with a product that was cheaper—one that created brighter, more colorful pictures. While some experts agreed they were photographically inaccurate, many consumers and customers liked them better. A giant retailer put the new competitive film on the shelf and people bought it. It seemed like Kodak never saw it coming.

The point is, our expertise can get in the way. We may be so convinced that our technology or business model is better that we may misjudge what our customers are willing to buy. Our bet is that the same experts who would argue for Kodak's film superiority would also argue that consumers would never accept digital imaging.

- Professors may argue against online learning.
- Doctors may argue against urgent care clinics in Wal-Mart and the Minute Clinics at CVS.
- What do you—someone who is an expert—argue against?

When you start with your biases (e.g., no one will ever buy cheaper, brighter film; no one will ever go to a nurse practitioner to get an antibiotic for a sinus infection), innovation fails us.

So what is innovation anyway? Innovation occurs when:

1. There is a significant unmet need or insight,
2. A product, service or business model meets that need (or fulfills the insight), and
3. There is clear communication and a commercialization strategy that links No. 1 to No. 2.

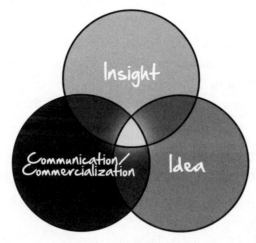

Meat Loaf may say "two out of three ain't bad." I respectfully disagree. Without all three in perfect alignment, the innovation will fail.

And if ever there were an industry in need of innovation, it is ours. While other industries have challenges, how many can you name (other than ours) with all of these?

- A product that is complicated and based on pooling of risks
- An aging distribution channel that is largely untrusted by the public
- A sales process that literally forces you to give blood and forces you to think about your own death or the death of someone close to you
- A sales decision process that rejects the people who are likely to want the product most
- Profit margins that are shrinking

No wonder the industry is having so much trouble.

I know. I know.

"Our business is more complicated than other businesses."

"Our products are accredited...regulated...more sophisticated...."

"Son, you don't really understand how much it takes to sell our product...."

After two decades of creating new products and services, I now recognize these kinds of reactions from "experts" as a symptom of unenlightened – often frightened – leadership. I've heard this language in every mature industry, and it always comes from an executive who is holding on to what used to work.

The good news? The incredible possibilities that this type of thinking creates *for those who don't share it.*

You can't cut your way into sustained profitability.

"Why go down the innovation path?" people sometimes ask. "Wouldn't it be simpler just to cut costs?"

The answer is: Yes, for a little while.

You certainly can reduce staff, slash expenses, slow down R&D, or reduce your investment in talent management and development. But the best leaders know that cutting is not effective in the long run.

The logical (sustainable) answer to growing margins is to raise prices. But in a commoditized business, it only works when everyone does it. When a few competitors raise their prices, a lot of the business goes to the others who don't...unless there is something truly differentiating the firms with the higher prices.

You must give people a REASON to pay more for something. And that is why you need to innovate. Unless you develop something new, different and better, you will always be seen as a "me-too" provider, and that is never a place you want to be. It dooms you to low margins, high employee turnover and days that are not a lot of fun.

Where should we innovate? Well, that takes us to the most fundamental business question of all.

What is the industry really here for?

Harvard Business School Professor Theodore Levitt, back in 1960, captured one of the major challenges our industry is facing today. His now classic article *Marketing Myopia* begins this way:

Every major industry was once a growth industry. But some that are now riding a wave of growth enthusiasm are very much in the shadow of decline. Others which are thought of as seasoned growth industries have actually stopped growing. In every case, the reason growth is threatened, slowed, or stopped is <u>not</u> [emphasis in the original] because the market is saturated. It is because there has been a failure of management.

That failure is caused by what Levitt called "marketing myopia," which he defines exactly as you would expect. It's what occurs when company leaders define their mission too narrowly; it's a form of business nearsightedness or shortsightedness.

Levitt offered what are now a few classic examples:

Industry	Myopic Purpose	The Broader Purpose
Railroads	Train travel	Transportation
Hollywood	Movies	Entertainment
Oil Companies	Petroleum	Energy
Dry Cleaning	Safe, effective cleaning of wool garments	Making clothes ready to wear

On the flip side, he cites companies such as DuPont, Kaiser Aluminum and Reynolds Metals Company that have thrived for centuries by remaining thoroughly *customer focused* and evolved — in terms of the products and services they offered — **as the needs of their customers did.**

WHY EXPERTS ARE "IN THE JAR"

There is a great saying in the South:

"You can't read the label when you are sitting inside the jar."

And you can't innovate from there, either.

If you have been with a company for more than six months, it is time you realize something: You're stuck in the jar. The way you think about new ideas is distorted by the corporate container you find yourself working within.

How do you know you are in the jar? You hear at least one of the following:

"We've tested that idea. It didn't work." What idea exactly? People who are in the jar interpret ideas based on how they last saw them.

In their minds, when they hear about a scooter, they think skateboard, not Segway. When they hear about an auction, they think Sotheby's, not eBay. They have literally judged an idea before it has been re-envisioned by the brilliant people around them.

Silence. When your team is trying to brainstorm new ideas, the room gets eerily quiet. The reality is that they are probably desperately trying to be creative, but they keep seeing hurdles. They don't want to appear negative, so they decide to be silent and nod a lot.

"Yes, but..." Trying to be polite, people will just "but" other people's ideas to death. ("It is a really interesting idea you are proposing, but it will never work because....") This is usually not about intent—they really want to be helpful—but they are too busy thinking about regulatory issues, manufacturing issues, political issues, budgetary issues, legacy systems, compliance concerns, channel conflict...deadening their ability to be creative.

An idea for (yet another) safe line extension. Line extensions and evolutionary innovation should be a large part of your plan. But when that's all your team is producing, it probably means they have lost the ability to recognize big ideas, or worse, they no longer have the fortitude to push the rope up the hill. Even when senior management begs for revolutionary thinking, they already see the inevitably depressing outcome and say, "Let's just add a bell, a whistle or a benefit rider and move on."

"Huh?" If you are often asked by really smart consultants or newcomers to your company, "What in God's name are you talking about?" you're probably in the jar (e.g., "I know, let's offer an annuitized universal whole life disability policy."). Seems that after a few months in the jar together, we develop our own language. Often laced with industry-borne acronyms and pet names, like "check-o-matic" or "universal life." This strange way of communicating seeps into our customer and client communications and keeps our customers from recognizing great innovation.

Don't let your experience blind you to the possibilities all around you.

YOU NEED TO GET OUTSIDE THE JAR

So now that you see yourself in the jar, what do you do about it? Here are three simple tips:

1. Get experts **from outside your industry** to examine your problem, preferably those who have faced a similar challenge. For us, that could mean telecom. They are fraught with regulation and commoditization and yet they have figured out how to keep adding revenues. How about pharma? They made some bold moves in the area of communicating benefits to consumers directly.

2. Get outside your office and act like an anthropologist. Spend time with your customer and bring an expert interpreter and a couple members of your team. Compare notes; you will be shocked at how differently you all see the situation. Too often we go just to our agents/distributors for new ideas. Remember, they are in the jar, too.

3. Be very careful about the language you use. In this case, "voice of the customer" should be taken literally. Customers recognize, respond to and build from their own words more than yours. So use their language when exploring insights, writing concepts and introducing new products. (More on this in Chapter 10.)

So some 50 years later, what can the insurance industry learn from this? Facing significant scrutiny, regulation, commoditization and ho-hum growth, can our purpose be broadened before it's too late? Instead of defining what we do for a living as manufacturing and selling insurance products for lives, property, disability, health, dental, legal, and various and sundry "exotic risks," can we think bigger? I've heard many define it slightly more broadly as "protection," but could there be an even broader purpose?

We must stop thinking about what we sell and think more about who we sell to.

Who are the people we can help? Who are we missing?

What do these people REALLY need that we can provide?

Could it be a product? A service? A new business model?

Insurance companies, when you really think about it, are not just in the protection business. They are in the **"lifestyle continuity business"** — keeping the lives of individuals, businesses and families intact when the unexpected happens. Additionally, you could add that insur-

ance companies deal with the problems associated with the inevitable and/or risks as THE CUSTOMERS define them. And not just for themselves, but for their heirs and their heirs.

You can see that by broadening our business definition. It helps us to expand beyond what is offered today to create new possibilities and innovations for the future.

Using one example, *lifestyle continuity business*, what possibilities open up?

You can come up with your own list, and I encourage you to do so, but here are two ideas:

- **Pet products.** The amount of disposable income spent on pets, everything from toys to health care, is mind boggling. Spending in this category, which has been climbing at double-digit rates in recent years, is now estimated at $50 billion, and there is no reason to think that sales will fall dramatically any time soon. For example, just recently I saw that my hair salon is selling a line of dog shampoos that have been tested on humans, not animals. The point is, pets are enjoying a higher rank in the pecking order of family priorities. Wealthier people are leaving more and more of their assets to pet trusts. Yes, pet trusts. These are trusts for the benefit of their pet. The lesson is that the feelings around pets create opportunity and high margins. Is there a way for insurance companies to consider pets a part of the family? Perhaps clauses that make it easier to direct benefit funds to pet care? Maybe offering incentives for leaving proceeds to animal rights organizations or veterinary hospitals? *(This is not, necessarily, a recommendation; it is just a little Fancy Feast for thought.)*

- **Divorce.** In the last couple of years, divorce rates fell, but not because of lack of irreconcilable differences. There are still plenty of those to go around…or sometimes go around twice or more. The reason why divorce rates fell was because of the economy. It's expensive to get divorced. Legal fees, the splitting of assets, etc. People were staying together for the sake of their pocketbooks.

And with the introduction of gay marriage comes gay divorce — a whole new industry where people of generally higher wealth are looking for expertise. Perhaps insurance companies can offer "promise insurance" as an alternative to a prenup. Maybe people would feel more comfortable getting amicably divorced if they knew they could still cover an ex-spouse in their employer's health plan. Maybe there could be more in the way of special considerations for people who are in a committed relationship but not married, thereby avoiding the need for divorce.

HOW TO RETHINK YOUR BUSINESS

A great way to rethink the business you are in is to start with the benefits you deliver to your customers and consumers.

For example, you may say you are in the informed solutions, education, providing qualified options, quick research, packaged choices, thought leadership...business.

If you do, you are in good company. When you Google these words, you'll find that, as defined by benefits delivered, you're in the same business as Orbitz, Amazon, Angie's List, WebMD and Edmunds.com. What could you learn from leaders in these businesses about innovative products and services?

What does all of this mean?

So how do insurance industry leaders harness the long-term trends that provide future opportunities? First, they must agree that change is needed. Not just evolutionary change, such as leveraging webinar technology to replace face-to-face meetings, or accepting premium payments online. I am talking about substantive change designed to produce annual double-digit sales and earnings growth.

Then they must commit resources to it. Money, yes, but also, and more important, the dedicated time and energy of some key thinkers in their organization. And they must have a good process for gaining the needed insight, developing an excellent idea pipeline, and communicating those ideas so that the market is ready for them.

WHY DO YOU WANT TO PAY MORE IN TAXES THAN YOU HAVE TO?

You are likely paying an innovation deficit tax. Why? Because **marketing and advertising are the tax you pay for a bad idea**. More accurately said, they have become the tax you pay for not being able to create a better idea than your competitors.

The days are gone when a nice tagline or clever campaign could create sustained buying behavior. The more complicated the product, the more likely that people will tap their social network to make decisions. People don't talk about ad campaigns when making these decisions. They share excitement and information about truly differentiated products. The lesson? The smartest companies are shifting their ad spend to innovation spend. They have realized that they can get exponentially higher return by investing in something that is truly different and needed, and THEN marketing it. And when they do, they spend less on marketing because their consumers do the marketing for them.

If you're considering spending a bunch of money on marketing or social media, why not start by developing a game-changing idea first and marketing it second?

But, most important, the attitude for change must be present. While it is easy to see change as a threat, the bigger threat you face is the loss of opportunity that will come by not changing. I am absolutely positive the world's biggest maker of buggy whips really did not want to change the things that made them number one. But, as it turned out, the risk of changing was smaller than the risk of becoming extinct.

Innovation has not been a core strength of our industry recently. Going forward, it will need to be. A key part of that innovation will be using emotion and customer involvement to change how our products and services are perceived. That is where we turn our attention to next.

Things to do Monday morning:

☐ Consider your current list of new initiatives. Look at each one and determine whether or not it is really an innovation. Is there a real (outside-the-jar) insight? Does the idea satisfy it? Is it easy to understand? Unless all three elements are present, it is not an innovation.

☐ Ask yourself the question: "What business are we really in?" Try to define it more broadly than the product.

☐ Think about your employees and salespeople and what they are saying about why your market share isn't bigger, sales aren't higher and/or profitability isn't great. Consider asking someone who is "outside the jar" the same question and compare the answers.

CHAPTER 2

Afraid of commitment? The vital roles of engagement and emotion

The first rule of business is the same as the first rule of life: Adapt or die.

In Chapter 1, I explained why our industry has to change. The obvious question is how?

The answer is not by coming up with a better business model or cutting costs. It is by fundamentally altering the way we position and communicate our products. We need to recognize that our first job is not just to create a new thing or a new way to buy; it is to get the consumer emotionally engaged with our products.

They were, when insurance was a new idea. But like many great relationships, the emotion has faded over time.

We need to get it back.

I spend a lot of time talking to industry executives, and I hear a common theme: "We just don't know what will be the best way to deliver our products in the future."

The people telling me this, probably like you, have tried many different things, with the approaches ranging from "expensive" to the "expensiver." Face-to-face is effective but not always efficient. Online is efficient but not always effective. Direct to consumer causes angst inside the management ranks because of the threat of channel conflict (and the threats by distributors to stop doing business with us).

FOUR OUT OF FIVE DENTISTS...

Many industries make the mistake of getting their insights from their distribution experts. Many years ago our company was helping P&G develop new oral health care products.

At the time, four out of five dentists recommended Crest. Many of these same dentists did not see whitening products as necessary or saleable. Why? Because they were in the oral health business, and whitening your teeth doesn't make your mouth healthier.

But the market had shifted. Consumers didn't care about gums; they wanted fresh breath and bright smiles. It was consumers—not dentists—who drove new product development in oral care.

When it comes to innovation, it turns out four out of five dentists can be wrong. Who are your dentists?

The results of all of this are predictable. Often the people charged with making each new innovation a reality procrastinate because they think they are just going to be wasting their time. ("Nothing is going to change.") And that puts smaller companies in a position to steal share.

So where should we start our change efforts once we know that things must indeed change?

It does not begin with creating a new product or business model. The place to start is with emotions – specifically, making sure that our customers are emotionally engaged with our products and services.

You want to create what I call "the involvement factor." That is, you want customers to interact with you in some way on a regular basis, even if it is not directly related to the core product, service or buying something new.

Most types of insurance are low involvement products. There is no reason for a customer to engage unless the customer is forced to (i.e., having to buy life insurance as a legal requirement or as part of a divorce settlement), or it is time to pay the quarterly premium. This is in stark contrast to a product like the iPhone – something that a consumer loves interacting with, and does so regularly. Insurance is also generally associated with negative emotions.

By way of context, it may be helpful to look at insurance and other products and services as plotted in the table, with the horizontal axis being the "involvement level" and the vertical one the emotion associated with the reason for engaging.

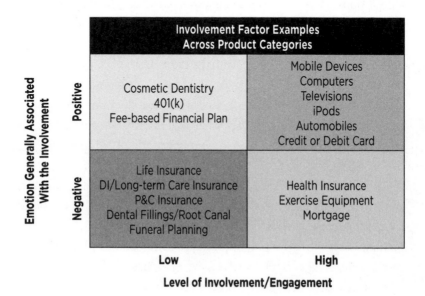

Anything that has both low involvement and negative emotion falls in what I call a "crisis category" — a place where emotions are negative and involvement is low. This is never a good place to be.

EMBRACE THE HATERS

The head of innovation at Kraft, Barry Calpino, recently helped me write a *Forbes* article called **Embrace the Hate to Innovate**. The premise is that too many companies focus on customers who love their services, and the companies try to give customers more of what they love.

The article argues that it is the people who HATE what we offer—both inside and outside our companies—that provide the greatest insights and, in turn, the biggest opportunities to create market-shaking, profitable innovation. You can learn many things from people who agree that you are in the crisis category.

You have to move the needle on one or both of those dimensions, otherwise your sales efforts are going to be the equivalent of flirting with the uninterested.

Note that these examples are just to offer a framework for thinking. Obviously, some of these categories will be placed in different boxes based on the consumer's individual emotions and situation. But the point here is that **spending money on increasing awareness is not enough** because you are literally flirting with the uninterested. You need to figure out ways to get consumers emotionally involved – in a positive way.

Not so long ago, they were. If you dial back the clock on the insurance category by several decades, back when our industry was growing, it may have landed in or nearer to the upper right quadrant. Why? Because of the debit system.

Before direct billing and online payments were available, agents came to the door each week to collect what was owed. They often stayed for coffee and had a pleasant conversation with the people who paid the premiums. That dynamic put the product into the space of higher involvement, and brought about more positive emotions associated with that involvement. (Chances are, the leadership in your organization remembers, and maybe even longs for, this type of engagement. But just like doctors making house calls, the times and behaviors have changed.)

While I am not suggesting that we recreate the debit system, perhaps there is another way to move insurance into a higher involvement, less negative space. Perhaps we could take a lesson from a cosmetic dentist. How did some dentists make the transition from being resisted to having people want to come in? By rewarding them with feeling better about themselves; by giving them whiter teeth and a nicer smile. It's no longer about filling the holes in your teeth; it's about filling the holes in your self-esteem.

Here's an example much closer to home involving an insurance geek (c'est moi) who did an experiment with some underinsured friends who knew they needed to buy life insurance but were put off by the thought. I tested the idea of making the experience more pleasant by holding a paramedical party one morning, in anticipation of the paramedical exam

we all would have to go through to get our policies. We all got up early, did not eat (since we were not supposed to), and had the technician come to my house, take blood and urine samples and applications from all of us. We laughed at ourselves for the newfound "closeness" we shared. He left; then we had bagels and mimosas. Much more pleasant and fun than a typical experience.

Weird, yes. Effective... yes!

Think about it.

Things to do Monday morning:

☐ Identify your most desirable target. They may just be the ones who hate you the most.

☐ Locate their areas of greatest involvement with your current products and services.

☐ Create three hypotheses for each area of involvement about how emotion could be more positive. Or, more specifically, think about the things the customer absolutely HATES. The greater the emotion, the more powerful the ideas will be.

☐ Test to see if you are right, à la my "insurance party" example. I thought if I made the process slightly more fun, people would be more willing to sign up — and I was right.

☐ Treat your team to some mimosas for trying to figure this stuff out. Innovation should be fun. **(More on that later.)**

CHAPTER 3

My stuff. My money. My self. The insurance pecking order

I think what we sell is pretty great.
Consumers? Not so much.
And therein lies an opportunity.

In the previous two chapters, I've talked about how consumers are not that into us. Now, let's dig a little deeper to find out exactly why.

According to a 2011 study done by Maddock Douglas, a strong majority of consumers acknowledge the importance of insurance, and this is true across categories — auto, home, health and life insurance. So despite low levels of involvement and negative emotion associated with the products, there is still a perceived need.

You can see that that's true in the following chart where we also asked about investments. But the perceived degree of importance is what varies a bit by category.

PERCEIVED IMPORTANCE OF HAVING VARIOUS KINDS OF INSURANCE/INVESTMENTS

Q. How important do you think it is for you to have each of the following?

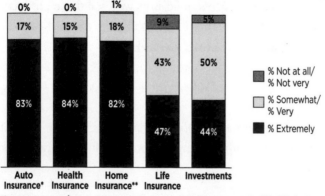

*Among car owners/leasers   **Among homeowners   Note: Figures may not add to 100 due to rounding.

This is where I see the need for pecking order emerging. It appears consumers are willing to insure their stuff, like cars or homes, more than their lives. Granted, auto insurance is mandatory in most states, and homeowner's insurance is often required to get a mortgage. Still, from an importance standpoint, it appears as though consumers are more willing to insure their stuff than themselves.

Let's break this down further. Do you think it is the product itself or the people interacting with it that is causing more negativity?

We asked consumers how positively or negatively they generally felt about each of the various insurance products as well as the agents and advisors they dealt with.

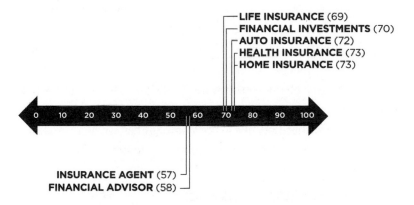

As you can see, they did not feel very positively about these products and even less so about the agents or advisors who sell these products. When I was in school, if I came home with a 69, that meant I got a D. (Parents dislike D's. Investors hate them.)

So we're seeing the products rated in the low C's and the agents and advisors – and again I am talking about the averages here – getting failing grades.

In addition to this overall perception, consumers indicate a lot of frustration and confusion, with as many as a fourth saying that they think insurance is a scam!

30%

"Policies are too complicated for a regular person to understand."

20%

"I'm not confident in my ability to choose the coverage plan that's right for me."

That's a big, strong, ugly statement. However, I feel it comes from not knowing and not understanding versus it actually being that bad. When I get a big book to explain everything I need to know about something that is not that interesting in the first place, I feel like the company is trying to CYA. Similarly, if I receive a document with a lot of fine print, I think the company sending it to me has something to hide. The more consumers feel that the product is complicated, the more they will feel they are buying something they don't need, being oversold or being cheated.

Wait. It gets worse.

All this is bad.

But what about the things your customer is not saying?

Our research experts at Maddock Douglas developed an interesting method for getting at people's unarticulated feelings and emotions. They used a series of 24 different paintings and asked respondents to choose the ones that best described their feelings before, during and after they purchased any kind of insurance.

The results were very interesting. The number one painting chosen to depict the feelings people had when they were getting ready to enter

the insurance purchase process was "The Scream" by Edvard Munch. Their open-ended comments indicated that they had very high anxiety and frustration while engaged with the product. That may not surprise you. But it is an opportunity to innovate.

Let's get personal.

In our research, we also asked more than 400 consumers in each product category about how they felt about the agents involved in the sale.

PERCENT OF CONSUMERS WHO DESCRIBE AGENTS/ADVISORS AS…

Q. Think of the last agent you encountered. Now please read the list below, and select each of the adjectives that could be used to describe that agent.

	Total %	Auto %	Home %	Health %	Life %	Investments %
Nice	46	54	56	32	37	40
Straightforward	45	51	52	27	37	41
Approachable	40	48	48	22	28	39
Accommodating	35	44	46	23	29	30
Confident	34	35	36	13	28	39
Intelligent	34	35	36	16	26	41
Trustworthy	33	39	38	16	27	34
Smart	30	28	28	17	25	34
Caring	28	34	36	17	24	24
Consultative	26	27	28	19	18	32
Unbiased	22	17	16	8	12	15
Successful	20	21	20	8	16	26
Traditional	19	27	29	11	18	14

> than "Total"

< than "Total" Significant differences at the 90% confidence level compared to "Total" are highlighted

As you can see, in the auto and home insurance categories, agents are much more likely to be described as nice, straightforward, approachable and accommodating—especially when compared to health insurance agents that consumers have dealt with. Financial advisors are more likely to be described as intelligent, smart, consultative and successful. In the life category, less than 30 percent of those consumers described their life insurance agents as approachable, confident, intelligent and trustworthy, and less than 20 percent were described as consultative and successful.

It was a little counterintuitive that the auto and home categories scored better than the other categories because the mandatory nature of the product could potentially make it more of a transactional feel. However, if you think about it a little deeper, the nonmandatory product categories, like life insurance and health insurance, have been continually moving "up market," classifying their clients as A's and B's and C's and D's—and just like in high school, you want to get as many A's and B's as possible. But since there are more potential customers who are C's and D's than A's and B's, it isn't surprising that the C's and D's are not feeling the love, since agents are spending less time with them or none at all.

All this bad news is really good news for innovators. Entrepreneurs have a pretty easy time getting a foothold in industries where there is a lot of consumer dissatisfaction because there are plenty of things they can fix with a new product, service or business model.

Conversely, they have a very difficult time competing within industries where satisfaction is incredibly high. Why? Because everyone is so happy with the way things are going they aren't interested in alternatives; there are fewer unmet needs to solve.

So here's a quick test: Do you find the previous charts depressing and annoying, or do you find them inspiring? If you find them depressing or if they annoy you, then you may be stuck in the jar. You're likely to look for ways to keep things the same rather than create new alternatives. If you find the charts inspiring, you have a creator's mindset; you understand exactly what it is going to take to change the future of the industry. Where others see obstacles and bad data, you see opportunities.

Summing up

So, look what is going on. A significant amount of life insurance con-sumers say that they don't feel all that engaged with their insurance com-pany, and a large percentage are telling us they don't feel confident in their ability to choose the right coverage plan (in large part because they don't understand their policies in the first place).

And they are communicating quite clearly that we are not as big a help to them as they would like.

In other words, we have tangible proof that they are not engaged with our product. They are just not that into us.

To all of you who say, "Well, you can't expect anyone to get excited about insurance," I point you to the website RealAge.com. You answer a bunch of questions and then hit the button and it calculates your "real age." If, for example, you are actually 41 but some of your answers show you as having a greater mortality risk (such as smoking or not wearing a seat belt), the website might list your real age as 46. People are very

engaged around this idea. Some 25 million people have visited the site. The concept of "age rate up" (or down) was actually invented by the insurance industry that, in the days before computers, added a couple of years to someone's real age if he or she were a smoker, or if there was only one rate table, deducted a couple of years from a woman's age to adjust for the fact that women live longer.

What's really clever about RealAge is that it creates a conversation around vitality, which results in the sharing of highly personal information about health, emotional and relational issues. This, in turn, exposes dozens of opportunities for the delivery of products and services, which are implicitly targeted. Sounds a lot like the "good old days," when an agent was sharing a cup of coffee with his client who was also his friend.

The success of RealAge was not surprising since we have all kinds of actuarial information. However, a bunch of doctors figured out a way to capitalize on it as they did with RealAge.

What other data do insurance companies have that could be interesting to consumers? Well, let's think of a few examples of industries that turned inward data outward.

Years ago, one of our clients, Allstate Insurance, recognized through the course of their innovation journey that consumers were not just coming to their website for education; they wanted to be "better prepared." That is, they wanted as much information as possible about what things cost locally so they could have an informed conversation with their insurance agent or knew how to judge the information on the company's website. That is ultimately how Allstate's Premium Gauge^{SM} tool was invented. It took the average claims experience in each zip code and translated it into English so that users could see why certain areas have higher rates than others. Armed with this information, they were emotionally prepared to engage in a discussion with any insurance company. But Allstate got the credit for helping them prepare and subsequently more business.

What else can we think of?

How about *The Biggest Loser*? Could an insurance company get involved in sponsoring, or offering, the tools that are used to evaluate

people who are looking to completely reshape their bodies? ("And now we go to the Body Mass Index calculator sponsored by Nationwide.") Now THAT is engagement. The public can't get enough of anything that will make them more attractive.

And don't overlook the intersection of behavior, big brands and technology. We now expect our cars to get us to our destination while the car is having a "conversation" with our insurance company about our driving, rewarding us with lower rates when we drive safely. Weight Watchers is combining its behavioral expertise with iPhone apps that scan and monitor food labels and has introduced technologies from companies like Body Media that actually track exactly what we're doing daily so we can modify our eating and exercise habits. We used to feel like our information was private. Now we get mad when our technology — and the brands we trust — are too stupid to anticipate what we need.

Think about this for a second. How many times in the past did you find yourself in a heated debate about privacy? Were you aware that consumer behavior had changed the conversation so quickly?

So what should we take away from all of this? If I got my wish, it would be that we are open to the idea that the engagement and emotion of our products can be improved. And we wouldn't succumb to "it is what it is." (One of my least favorite phrases, by the way.) If we can believe that consumers find our products important enough to be frustrated by them, then there is hope. However, we need to consider how our process, our product and our people are affecting their experience, and determine what we can do about it to make it substantially better.

Things to do Monday morning:

☐ Think about the process by which consumers acquire our products. Break it down to tiny component parts, but from a layman's perspective. Rebuild it as though the product never existed. What would it look like if it were invented today, and not built off of old "stuff." (See Part 5 for a few examples.)

☐ Think about the things you already have, use and/or are developing that have any element that may be interesting to consumers. Something they would love to "play with" because it helps them learn more about their favorite subject – themselves. Can you think of anything? If not, consider asking your employees if there are assets that they routinely play with or would want to just for fun.

☐ Analyze your training programs. Is there anything you can do to help agents with how they are perceived by consumers? Today's training programs focus on the sale. But how many focus on skill building that will help them to just be better communicators? Maybe it's tone of voice. Maybe they need to take a comedy class or two. Perhaps it is a lesson in listening skills. Are we afraid to tackle those issues? I hope not.

☐ Consider partnering with another brand or company that can create a 1 + 1 = 5 result. Who has the technology, brand or channel that will allow us to become more fun, relevant and effective?

CHAPTER 4

Infusing emotion (safely): Avoiding the "ick" factor

Now that you're convinced that you need to get consumers emotionally involved with your products, the question becomes which products are ripe for this approach and how do you do it effectively? The last thing you want to do is invoke an "ick" factor.

Emotion, as anyone who has ever been in a relationship knows, is a tricky thing. Sure, there are the rainbows, puppies, "no, you hang up first"s, and the "I love you more than life itself"s....

But emotional relationships also come with bad moments. In the aftermath of a fight, you might hear, "I never want to see your ugly face again"...and worse.

When it comes to products with emotions, there may be no more tricky ones than viaticals, where someone sells their life insurance policy to a third party. In the past, it was most common with terminally ill or very sick people. Now it is becoming more of a regular thing among seniors (called life settlements).

It is easy to describe how these transactions work. The buyer estimates the life expectancy of the seller and offers him the present value of the death benefit, minus the profit he would like to make.

You can see why someone would be tempted to sell. If the death benefit of a policy were $1 million, for example, and the cash value of that policy was $400,000, the policyholder would only get $400,000 if he or she needed the cash right away. However, if a potential buyer did a life expectancy calculation and found out that the policyholder was only expected to live for about three more years, the buyer might offer the person $600,000 today for the likelihood of receiving $1 million in about 36 months.

The seller gets cash, while he or she is alive, and the buyer, if the actuarial tables are right, receives a higher return than he or she could have received by investing elsewhere, once the seller dies. (**Making 66 percent on your money for a three-year period, as you would in this example, is an extremely good deal to say the least.**)

Why all the interest?

With savings accounts paying little in interest, longer life expectancies and general economic turmoil, many older people are looking for sources of cash. Life insurance policies are so misunderstood that it is easy to see how some people would look to this asset as the "first to sell" as they search for ways to raise money. (**Whether or not it is in their best interests is a topic for another book. Working title: Nest Egg Omelets.**)

On the buy side, investors like the lack of correlation between viaticals and the performance of stocks, bonds and real estate. The return on the investment depends primarily on the accuracy of the life expectancy (LE) calculation and has nothing to do with how the financial markets are performing or not performing.

Win/win or win/lose/lose?

On the surface, it looks like a good deal all around. Someone who needs the money gets it immediately (while he or she is still alive), and the investor gets a superior return.

But if you look a little closer, you find there are all kinds of problems, and ironically the "ick" factor, which comes from investing in the death of strangers, is not the biggest one. In fact, the ick factor didn't exist at all when viaticals were invented in the 1980s. Then the people receiving the money were almost exclusively those dying from AIDS, and the industry was seen in a positive light for providing money to people who could live out their lives with dignity.

But since then, these arrangements have morphed into purely financial arrangements where the net result is not win/win, but win/lose (**and lose again, as we shall see**).

Today, the transaction is simply seen as a bet where someone is right and the other wrong. The buyer is betting that the seller won't live as long as he or she thinks – the quicker the seller dies, the greater the buyer's return – and the seller is betting the buyer is wrong in estimating when the seller will die.

Either way, the insurance company is a sure loser (the second lose, in the win/lose/lose equation). The insurance company had already made a bet that a certain number of these policies would lapse before death benefits were paid out, and it has now lost that bet because all of these policies will remain in force until death.

So back to "ick"

All mathematical analysis aside, how does this feel from a social responsibility point of view? The answer is not great. The life insurance industry was created, in the words of the lawyers, "to help people with an insurable interest in another person hedge the financial risk of his or her death." In plain English, a person who has life insurance on another needs to want that person to live long, not die soon. Laws were created to ensure that people could not take policies out on strangers and then kill them for the money. It is that morbidly simple.

So why now is it OK to own life insurance on someone you don't even know? It's because of a loophole based on rules that were created a long time ago, which had companies policing insurable interest only at the time of inception, not upon transfer.

But no matter how viaticals or life settlements came into being, there seem to be many more options the industry could be offering older people – options that could actually result in a win/win/win.

The opportunity for entrepreneurs and innovators

Knowing that there is a need for seniors to have additional sources of cash, wouldn't it make sense for insurance companies to reclaim this space? (The banks are already here through reverse mortgages, and the

life settlement companies own the viaticals.) Suppose they invented an option to "re-underwrite" people at an advanced age and recalculate their life expectancy. Perhaps they would make an offer to buy them out of their life insurance early, especially if their health situation had changed.

For example, suppose a $1 million policy was issued a while ago when the person was 65 and healthy. Then, five years later, when there was $400,000 of cash value in the policy, the person's health suddenly declined and he or she was expected to die within three years.

For the insurance company, that is a death claim of $1 million in three years. If it had the ability to re-underwrite, it might offer the person $600,000 ($200,000 more than the cash value) in order to avoid paying $1 million three years from now, or sooner (should the person not live as long as expected).

If the person really needs cash now — to pay for medical expenses, for example, or just wants to take a trip around the world — he or she would have the option of getting more than the contract allowed for at the moment, and the insurance company gets a chance to minimize its losses. From the customer's point of view, no one is waiting for him or her to die.

While this may not be as sexy on paper as life settlements, it would put insurance companies in a far better light. The settlements would be marketed by saying to customers, "We know you need/want the money, and we can give you more than your cash value."

And there would be no "ick" factor.

This would be a great example of moving from a "What" business to a "Who" business, and it's a great time to illustrate another point. There are often multiple "who"s involved in a decision. For example, in the case of aging parents, the children are important influencers. They need to be understood just like the parent/policyholder. While working with GE Medical, we found that it was the children's desire to live rich, full lives that actually drove a valuable product development for the parents who were aging at home. If we'd focused just on the parents we would have missed the mark and missed the opportunity to improve the lives of seniors.

This would be one way to increase the positive emotions associated with our products. And there are other opportunities as well. The key is remembering that you don't always have to make it about the product per se, but about the experience. For example, how do your customers feel when they go to your website? Is it clear? Is it confusing? Is it entertaining? What about your advertising and product literature? Does it make you want to throw it away immediately? Read it? Save it but not read it? More about this later (in Chapters 9 and 10) when I talk about language and unclaimed touch points.

Things to do Monday morning:

- ☐ Consider the features and benefits of the product(s) you are marketing. Reconsider any that rely on loopholes in the law in order to be effective. If there is an obvious loophole, you could have "ick" on your hands.

- ☐ Consider the emotions used in crafting your marketing message. Are any of them designed to make one feel purposefully negative about oneself? While you may suggest that this is a requirement to sell a "sold, not bought" product, I suggest you consider testing the effectiveness with different segments against messages that are either more upbeat, humorous or otherwise positive.

- ☐ Don't be afraid to ask for regulatory change. If the idea doesn't neatly fit into current laws, yet the need is real, it may be worth putting your government affairs team to work.

- ☐ As you move to considering "who" you are selling to instead of "what" you are selling, make sure that you deeply understand the needs of *all* the influencers as well.

Part 2

PUSH OR PULL?

CHAPTER 5

Distribution-centricity: It's a major problem

Pushy salespeople, lack of trust, imbalance of power in the supply chain and other generally outdated techniques all characterize the distribution systems in crisis categories like insurance. In fact, the power is so out of balance that many companies characterize their distributor as their customer.

Here I examine the intended and unintended consequences of models that put the power – and role of insight development – in the hands of distributors.

There is a wonderful opportunity right in front of all of us in the insurance industry. The trouble is our glasses are dirty.

In a business that is so distribution focused – or in hipper terms, "B2B" oriented – it is not only convenient to ask producers and agencies for input before launching a new product, service or business model, it's imperative. However, many companies stop there. They don't talk to the people who actually buy the product – the consumer (which for some reason we keep calling the policyholder, as if our customers are different from those who decide to buy at one supermarket versus another or different from those who decide to buy a Honda instead of a Toyota).

Sometimes when companies decide not to reach out to the consumer, it is because they don't want to spend money on consumer research – since the agent is controlling the sale anyway. Sometimes it is because distributors feel threatened when companies go to consumers directly. And sometimes it is because they just don't think they will learn anything new.

R.I.P. B2B

I was recently in a meeting with the president of a $2 billion B2B business. It was our first meeting. Moments into it, and completely unprompted, I was surprised when he said, "Let's face it. B2B is dead."

The reason his comments surprised me wasn't because I don't agree with the statement—I do—but because his company controls more than 80 percent of the market in which his four different product categories participate. More important, much of his revenue comes from other companies that buy his products and then resell them under different brand names.

So why would he make such a surprising statement? His point was that he could not trust his buyers to drive innovation. They did not know what their consumers wanted. To drive innovation, his firm had to know more about consumers than his customers did.

It's as simple as this: He who best understands the consumer wins every time—period.

What's interesting is that the more the industry matures, the less validity there is to any of these arguments—particularly in the case of Millennials (aka Gen Y who, as I said, are children of the baby boomers). Here there is more and more disconnect between what the industry does and how it is relevant to these younger consumers.

So notice what is going on. Our sales channels are becoming more and more disconnected from the needs of our customers. Is it because they don't understand them? Is it because there is no margin in selling them what they think they need? Is it because they filter their needs through outdated understandings? Yes. Yes. Yes.

In Chapter 10, I am going to talk a lot about language. But suffice it to say for now, the industry says one thing and Gen Y hears something else.

Not surprisingly then, a study by Competiscan, a company that compiles competitive marketing data, shows there is a big disconnect between the way that salespeople and corporate executives feel about their company advertisements and literature and the way consumers do. Of 12 companies' literature analyzed, consumers consistently gave lower

scores than agents did when it came to clarity, reassurance and likelihood of doing business.

So what is the opportunity? Perhaps it is time to examine these issues deeply from the perspective of the consumers and the influencers around them so that new conclusions can be drawn, and new ideas can be developed. This is the high-level definition of what it means to be insight driven — a "Who" business. Additionally, having someone else outside your industry interpret the results will give you a valuable perspective. (See Chapter 18.)

Anyone have any lens cleaner? Let's get started.

Under-banked, under-insured or just under-understood? How innovation may have prevented the flight from middle market

As I think about what is happening in the banking world post the credit crisis, the economic meltdown and Financial Regulatory Reform, it is hard not to think about the impact on the everyday consumer.

Banks could lose significant fee revenue as a result of caps on fees post-FinReg. They have to figure out a way to make it up. They are likely to go where the money is — up market.

Even before FinReg, a large proportion of consumers were "unbanked," relying on check cashing services instead of traditional banks for their everyday needs. While these services are often far more expensive, they are often better trusted and, equally important, far more accessible to the people who use them.

A recent *Wall Street Journal* article included this intriguing chart. The majority of unbanked households are in what would be labeled racial minority groups. However, they are also, according to the U.S. Census Bureau, the fastest-growing segments of the population.

UN-ACCOUNTED FOR U.S. Households without a savings or checking account

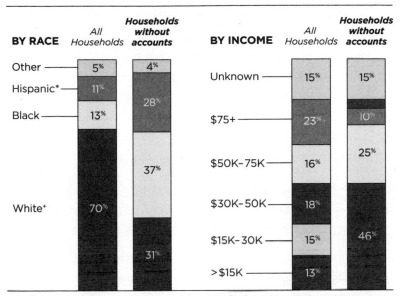

BY RACE	All Households	Households without accounts
Other	5%	4%
Hispanic*	11%	28%
Black	13%	37%
White⁺	70%	31%

BY INCOME	All Households	Households without accounts
Unknown	15%	15%
$75+	23%	10%
$50K–75K	16%	25%
$30K–50K	18%	46%
$15K–30K	15%	
>$15K	13%	

Note: Figures may not add to 100 due to rounding. *Not Black +Neither Black nor Hispanic
Source: Federal Deposit Insurance Corp and Census Bureau Survey of 54,000 households
with 86% responding.

Yet despite this, insurance companies are following the same path as the banks. They also have moved up market because that's where they think the money is. And they are right...for the moment.

But as a result, the middle and lower ends of the market are being underserved – dramatically underserved when we are talking about the low end – and emphasis has been on finding the product that cracks the code. Simplifying underwriting by eliminating some of the medical tests before offering insurance has driven the price too high to buy. (After all, we need to raise rates to compensate for the lack of information.) And selling the current product is unprofitable in lower amounts. (A policy that breaks even at $200,000 in coverage is a money loser at $100,000.)

But is product the key? Perhaps there is something else that could be innovated in order to help the market understand the benefits of dealing with insurance companies. Check cashing services are not part of Wal-Mart's core business, yet they offer the service to attract the unbanked

into their stores. Telecom companies are not really in the wire transfer business, but they allow you to "text" small amounts to charity. ("**Text HAITI** to the number 90999.") Perhaps the missing components here are:

- **The right mindset:** We need to figure out how to reach this market.
- **The right research:** What product/service can we provide relatively easily that is even vaguely related to what we do?

No book on innovation is complete without an Apple example. So ask yourself this question: "Which recording executive thought Apple had a chance to be successful in the music business?" If you find one, please let me know. I don't blame them for not taking Apple seriously. After all, the music companies had the contracts, the talent, the brands, the stores, the devices (e.g., the Sony Walkman and CD players).

But Apple found a need — portable data storage — and an unchallenged paradigm — you must buy a whole album — and BAM! A bunch of stunned, gray-haired executives got punched in the face by a completely different business model that served the masses. And let's not overlook that more music gets sold under this new model. Selling in smaller portions can often lead to much higher margins and sales.

The kind of research Apple did to come up with their music business went beyond demographics and geographics (i.e., where they live) and included attitudes, behaviors and beliefs.

The sustainability of our brands is going to depend on knowing where the makeup of the market will be 20, 30 or 50 years from now. If you don't feel you understand your market deeply, it may be time to take a step back and become a student again.

Things to do Monday morning:

☐ Stop looking to fire your consumer research team. If you don't see their value, it is because either you need to give them better direction or you need better people on the team. Consumer research is not an option. It is an imperative. (I will talk more about this in Part 4.)

☐ Invite someone from another industry to one of your staff meetings or product development meetings. Get his or her perspective on how the products and services feel.

☐ Become an anthropologist. Not really, but just one from the Barbizon School of Anthropology (where you can be an anthropologist or just look like one …). Get out and watch how real customers interact with your product in real time. Create your own personal, unbiased lens.

CHAPTER 6

Distribution paradigm shifting: Innovation or hallucination?

The earth is round. Man can travel to the moon. It is possible to run a mile in under four minutes. And insurance distribution models can be made efficient.

Which of these things is untrue? Well, the first three have been proven, and the last one has not, of course. However, all four have something in common. At one point, each was assumed to be impossible. Sailors were warned that they could fall off the edge of the earth if they went too far; space travel was considered something that could only happen in science fiction; and countless "experts" said the sub-four minute mile would never be achieved.

So I think there is hope when it comes to the way we distribute our products. But, I will concede, it does seem like a long shot. We seem stuck and, perhaps more important, I sense a steady lessening of interest and excitement to "get 'er done."

Over the last several decades (yes, decades), the insurance industry has been lamenting not only the decline of life insurance ownership in the U.S., but also the shrinking, aging and declining profitability of the face-to-face distribution channel. Attempts at modernizing this channel have not made much of an impact; attempts at growing it significantly have been unimpressive; and attempts at going direct are not really direct in most cases. There is usually a middleman getting paid, but he (or she) is on the phone or on the other side of the Internet connection.

Maybe the loss of steam I mentioned in the introduction to this chapter is coming from a sense of futility?

That is understandable. But do you think that Christopher Columbus, Neil Armstrong or Roger Bannister ever felt like giving up? Well, probably. But if any of them actually did give up, the world would be a different place.

So let's try viewing the problem from a different angle.

Most of us with any experience in the insurance world will look first at an offering and find fault with it, and then assume that those flaws are the reason it is so difficult to sell this stuff.

Well, those flaws could be the problem. But could there be something else going on to keep consumers from beating down our doors?

We may be too close to the problem to know. We need a different perspective. How about examining what is happening elsewhere in the world of sales? Not in sales of insurance, but in sales in general. A quick look around shows that consumer tolerance for certain approaches is changing – rapidly.

Sales gurus tell us that **the consumers' tolerance for push marketing is waning**. People like Wendy Weiss, "the queen of cold calling," and Jill Kornrath, author of *Selling to Big Companies*, say you can't just go out and figuratively knock on doors and people will buy. You have to know how to find who is looking for you already, otherwise they will not listen. If push marketing isn't dead, it is on life support.

Just to be sure we are all on the same page, let's make a distinction between push marketing and pull marketing. Push marketing is the type of activity that a company engages in to entice its sales force to sell more of a product. It includes things like sales incentives, awards and high commission rates. **With this approach, companies are essentially "pushing" the product from company to consumer through the distribution chain.**

Pull marketing, in contrast, is when a firm goes directly to the consumers and positions the product or service in such a way that entices them to ask for the product…to seek it out…to "pull" it from the company toward them.

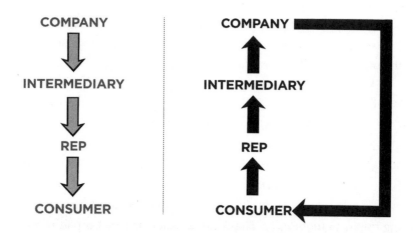

Obviously, the insurance industry relies most heavily on push activities to get the job done. And if we believe, as I do, that consumers are becoming ever less tolerant of push marketing, that, of course, could be a big reason we are having a problem with our sales efforts.

Perhaps the idea that the product must be "pushed" needs a second thought.

Let's see what has changed since the days when push marketing made sense. To keep people from getting defensive, let's look at the world of sales in general instead of just our industry.

Today's consumers are USING salespeople as information sources for validating decisions that they may have ALREADY "made." For example, Suze Orman might recommend that people stay away from annuities and whole life or that they buy gold. Then they will go to financial advisors who are telling them what they think they want or don't want. ("I don't want an annuity, and I want term insurance not whole life, and I want to buy gold.") In the past, prospects would use salespeople as the educators. Now they tell them what they want and ask the salespeople to give them good reasons why NOT to do that. The more complicated the buying decision is, the more likely that this behavior will take place. For example, people who buy cars regularly go on sites like Edmunds.com and then go to dealerships only to pick up

cars once the lowest price has been negotiated online. The salespeople are being marginalized and, in some cases, completely eliminated from the process by tools that validate the consumers' decisions.

There seem to be two clear conclusions we can draw from this:

1. Consumers have FAR less time for a pitch but plenty of time to surf the Web for what they are interested in.

2. Consumers must see/perceive some value in what you have to offer BEFORE they will even listen to you. They are way too busy to listen to a cold call.

So, basically, what this is telling us is that the consumers are selling things to themselves. This is not a hallucination; it is part of what Wikinomics calls the trend of prosumerism. A prosumer is a mashup between a consumer and one or more of the following: a professional, a producer of goods and services, and proactive behavior. This trend is the reason why revolutions in other industries such as photography, music production, law and publishing now allow individuals to cut out the professional altogether. Programs and websites like LegalZoom, GarageBand, Amazon's self-publishing unit, Shutterfly and others have allowed people to function as their own lawyer, record producer and publisher – eliminating (or, at the very least, severely lessening) the need for attorneys, recording studios and publishing houses. Yes, of course, there is still a place for those things, but they are taking up less and less room as the glut of unemployed attorneys, recording engineers and professional editors can attest.

Let's go back and look at the three trends to see why all these things are going on and how we might benefit from the changes that are now a permanent part of the selling landscape.

1. **Using salespeople as validation.** Obviously, we are not doing this well. We will need to change how we train salespeople to behave. They need to learn first how to make consumers feel good about themselves and the research they have done so that the salespeople are not reduced to an order taker but seen as having an important opinion in the process of making the decision.

("Yes, I understand why Suze Orman said term insurance is the way to go for most people, but in your case....") This will require us, of course, to be thoroughly aware of what advice is already out there. Instead of spending so much of your wholesaling budget helping agents see the difference between carrier A's and carrier B's products, how about giving them sales tips on how to deal with the information that prosumers are likely going to use to make a decision. It won't be about another brand; it will be about another alternative. And that alternative could be doing nothing.

2. **Less pitching, more surfing.** To capitalize on this trend will require our sales presentations to be geared toward what people have likely seen online. In addition, they will have to be shorter and to the point. Is the change possible? Sure. But it will require a deep understanding of what your demographic is looking for online, as well as new techniques to enable your sales team to either say things more succinctly, or to capture attention for a greater length of time — perhaps both. The days of the lengthy needs analysis questionnaires for insurance may be numbered. It's not because taking in someone's whole picture isn't important; it's that today's younger consumers expect you to know them already. That sounds like a hallucination, too, but today's technology makes it possible. Face it — boomers taught their Gen Y kids that they are the center of the universe. It worked. We have to get with the program. If you can't find all their information that you need in advance, figure out a way to keep them entertained and interested long enough for you to get it face to face. (I swear, I think comedy classes will replace toastmasters in fewer than five years.)

3. **Establishing value before they will see you.** This requires some kind of relevant information flow directly to consumers before you meet or talk with them so that they agree there is a reason to interact with you. How much of our marketing, advertising and R&D budgets are aimed directly at the consumer to ensure this happens? Hint: Not much. Here is where training programs should take a chunk of money that is used today to help train agents to "smile and dial" and put it toward teaching them how to be thought leaders. Thought leaders establish themselves as experts in topics that are narrow and deep. They put information out online in an interesting, provocative and smart way, and people find them. That's what Suze did. She became the expert on helping young people get out of credit card debt, and then her thought leader reputation just blossomed from there. Your reps don't all need to have that kind of fame to be successful, but they need a similar path to stay relevant in the world of the prosumer.

When you look at these three points, it is clear there is a lot of work to be done. And the place to start is trying to figure out why consumers are doing all the work to sell products to themselves.

Well, it could be chicken or egg. Information has allowed consumers to be in control, OR it could be that a lack of innovation has caused them to go out looking.

It doesn't matter where you come out. The trend is real, and we need to capitalize on it—and we haven't. If we think about the most innovative, brilliant, attention-grabbing things that have occurred in the life insurance industry over the last few decades, the biggest high fives go to the inventions that squeeze more out for a lower price. Let's look at the "winners" (i.e., the ones that probably commanded the most revenue and awareness):

- Direct response term aggregators (let's put all the cheap products next to each other and watch them get cheaper)

- Secondary guarantee universal life products/guaranteed income annuities (because one appropriately priced guarantee apparently was not enough)
- Life insurance settlements (we will give you more than your insurance company—just die sooner, please)

The "C" word is coming to mind. Commodity. The consumers see insurance as a commodity. And as things stand now, they may very well be right—a conclusion I absolutely hate since it does not have to be true.

Why do the consumers see insurance as a commodity? It's because:

A. We haven't done anything new in a while to reinvent it or provide new value.

B. We've been focused on a shrinking market with the same products. We haven't done enough homework to know who needs something new that we could deliver.

And while you can point to products like cash value life insurance and say it is far from a commodity, my response is that not one person in 100 outside of the industry knows what it is. And that leaves the other 99 thinking that all insurance products are the same.

So is this a fait accompli? Are we doomed to be selling commodities? Well, if coffee (e.g., Starbucks) and water (e.g., Evian, which by the way is naïve spelled backward), arguably the ultimate commodities, can figure out a way to differentiate themselves and charge a lot of money, I think we can too. We are obsessed with making our products stand out in differentiating my term coverage from yours. But I sincerely believe we can do more than that. We can make our distribution model add value, as well.

Let's examine some opportunities, beginning with our sales force.

Know anyone who looks forward to talking to an insurance agent? Insurance salespeople are seen as another commodity. And the commodity has an extremely negative connotation. Here's a joke I never heard before—probably because someone would think I would be insulted by it, particularly because my husband started his career as an insurance agent—but, apparently, it is an old standby outside the industry:

A woman was in the hospital after feeling very ill.
The doctor says to her, "I have some bad news for you.
You only have three months to live."
"Oh, that's terrible," the woman sighs. "What am I going to do?"
The doctor replies, "Marry an insurance agent."
"Will I live longer?" asks the woman.
"No," replies the doctor, "but it will SEEM longer."

This may sting a bit, but there is another important lesson here: Pay attention to laughter. When you hear people giggle or snort around an idea, there is a core emotional reaction that should signal your leadership to pay attention. After two decades of product development, we have noticed that a majority of the biggest ideas literally started as jokes.

If a lot of people you tell that joke to end up laughing — and I think they will — it is confirmation that we have a problem — and a huge opportunity.

No wonder we have so much trouble attracting young people to the profession. If our potential salesmen and women view our industry as one that sells low engagement products containing negative emotion, they have very little reason to do this for a living. This is particularly true with a generation so focused on changing the world. (Wait, there is another opportunity!)

And we in the industry certainly aren't helping things. Here's something I've heard over and over in focus groups of young people who have just joined our companies as salespeople. These "newbie" or green pea agents repeatedly said, "I hate selling to my friends and family." (There is another opportunity!)

We make them do this. It's "the way it always has been done…gotta earn your stripes just like I did…." And it stinks. It's embarrassing. Mostly because it points to the fact that we haven't developed products or services that people want to buy. (Another opportunity!)

While it may have been easier 20 or 30 years ago to learn how to sell by doing this — and somehow I doubt that it was — times have changed. The image of the industry has deteriorated, and having our newest agents

sell to friends and family just makes everyone uncomfortable and perhaps is accelerating a declining perception.

Can we think of something better? Can we train them on business development instead of product pushing? In other words, if we take the focus off of the benefits and features of the product, and help them find people who are actually looking for what we have to sell, that would go a long way toward changing this for the better. We could show them how to partner with CPAs to reach high net worth clients looking for tax strategies; ways to find new parents in need of more insurance; or small businesses in need of succession planning help. Instead of telling them it is a good idea to target these people, let's train them in how to do it.

But not only can we change the way we train our sales force, we can change who they target, as well. And that brings us to our second uncomfortable question:

Are we racist? Sexist? Homophobic and lacking trust in the next generation? We are just dipping our toe into multicultural markets and other demographic segments. We don't know NEARLY enough about these segments to be effective, and yet we are quick to redirect resources away from them if they don't produce immediate results. I am talking here about the Hispanic, African American, Asian, women, Gen Y, GLBT (Gay, Lesbian, Bisexual, Transgendered) and special needs markets. This is a key distribution opportunity because these markets are not being served adequately, and they also represent a new source of recruits. Can we gain more insights and be a little more willing to test and learn?

The 2010 census shows what I thought we already knew; however, somehow it feels like news. There was a 9.7 percent increase in population and 50 percent of that was Hispanic. Families that have the highest birthrates seem like a logical choice to target life insurance sales, yet an increase in sales in these areas has not materialized to any great degree.

Yes, there are cultural differences that make the Hispanic market trickier; however, the fact is, we do not fully understand them. Companies feel comfortable with acculturated Hispanics, but there is little being done to target them specifically either. For the most part, if they are English

speaking, they are approached in the traditional way. But is this the best approach? This seems like an area that should require much more exploration and insight.

Maddock Douglas recently did some innovation work for a global retailer that focused on launching services currently available in the U.S. into other countries. What we found was that the needs of consumers changed dramatically from one country to another – not a big surprise. What WAS a bit of a surprise was how differently ethnic groups within the U.S. and other countries responded to different services. Even when people shared a national anthem, families with different cultural backgrounds wanted – and expected – completely different products and services.

There is also an unspoken (or softly spoken) fear of the multicultural market representing a bad risk. The cultural tendency to be more private with financial information and protective of family makes companies fearful that they will not tell the truth. That might be true, but can't we solve for that tension? Can't we build models to underwrite the risk like any other one? What other choice do we have?

When it comes to other segments, like women for example, many companies are taking steps such as developing special programs to hire more women agents, or to offer women-only events, but are internally frustrated by the results. From my observation, there has been a lot of starting, stopping and hitting the redo button instead of testing and learning from what does and does not work. We need to do a better job because traditional techniques are often seen as a turnoff to women.

For example, agents are taught to get the sale in as few meetings as possible. Many women see that as "wham, bam, sign here, ma'am." Women may need a longer time to digest and think about things before making a decision. They are put off by the pressure of having to decide on the spot. But that does not mean it requires women to sell to women; it just means that they need a certain kind of information exchange before they will make decisions. For example, they like to bounce the ideas off other people, perhaps their friends or colleagues. The industry is very impatient with this, and so they pull the plug on an extremely large seg-

ment of the market. As a result, we are not learning from what worked and what didn't. We must consider new models that do not expect a sale after a couple of meetings. Better yet, let's start a deep dive into research and discover insights that would tell us what to do.

Gen Y is also befuddling. My not-so-secret theory is that the ranks of insurance executives, mostly boomers, see Gen Y more as their children than they do potential customers. In other words, they look at members of Gen Y and see their kids — people who still need to be cared for and told what to do. Viewed that way, they conclude that Gen Y is not a good market for insurance because, to buy insurance, you need to be a responsible adult, and they don't see "their kids" that way, not to mention the fact that these kids don't have any money.

But that thinking is shortsighted. One day these "kids" will have the money. Actually, many do already. And as for the belief that Gen Y thinks insurance is irrelevant in their lives right now, I don't think that has to be the case. Did you know that the oldest Gen Yers are in the second half of their 30s and many are parents?

When young people are recruited into the life insurance industry, they get it. They buy policies for themselves. However, those young recruits are becoming fewer and further between. We must find ways to make insurance more relevant to Gen Y, which will give the industry the side benefit of the profession becoming more attractive, as well.

And GLBT? The industry sometimes confuses serving a need with promoting a lifestyle. This market is, on average, better educated and wealthier but is one that also has needs that are not always served by traditional rules governing insurance benefits and estate planning. So doing a lot more work to gain insight and develop ideas, and then promoting them in an appropriate way, makes a lot of sense. Let's lose the fear.

So the bottom line about all of this is that we need more insight. We don't know nearly enough to innovate in all of these markets that we are underserving.

Digging deeper

As long as I am asking questions, here's another one:

Are we torturing our consumers? We take their time, their blood, we make them pee in a cup, and answer all kinds of intimate and embarrassing questions, then we ask them for money, and then we make them wait – sometimes for weeks or months – to see if we are going to find them worthy. At the end of all that, they get life insurance – maybe.

A few years later – and we have only sent them a birthday card and maybe a calendar at Christmas in the interim – we call and ask them to do it again.

We know they need to go through each of the steps; it's important, but the process is barbaric. Anti-selection, which is the tendency for the worst insurance risks to seek insurance, is certainly an issue. However, if we need all that information, can't we at least have a party? Maybe serve some wine and cheese after the blood tests are over? Maybe bring in a band or a DJ? *(I am only partially joking. Mimosas anyone?)*

I am not suggesting we offer insurance to everyone who applies. I am just saying we need to figure out OTHER ways to make the experience better. It is a huge opportunity.

Are there models that can reach the middle-class market more effectively?

Think about possible distribution models that have been tried before: aggregation models, direct, one-to-many selling (payroll deduction).

Many have tried these in one form or another, but no one seems to have addressed the underinsured problem to any great degree. Truly direct models are seen as a potential threat to current face-to-face channels. But perhaps there are ways to look at this issue differently. Is it really a conflict? Are these channels really serving the same markets? Maybe there is other insight to be gained from research. The industry lacks good segmentation data and a true understanding of the attitudes and behaviors of the segments. Maybe there are channels that can create new roles for "agents"—roles that don't look like they do today, but are interesting,

valuable and productive nonetheless; roles where they behave like educators, business developers, marketers, coaches or social networking experts…or something else that customers and potential customers will find beneficial.

It is helpful to take lessons from other industries that have faced and/ or solved similar challenges. Pharma, for example, is a great one. Distribution through "push" was the way drugs were sold. But now consumers are asking for certain drugs by name. They are seeing ads on television. These create brand awareness for specific drugs and so they ask for them. If doctors are indifferent to brands that do the same thing as what they were going to prescribe, they give the consumers what they ask for. How can we capitalize on this?

EVERYTHING OLD CAN, INDEED, BECOME NEW AGAIN

Be careful not to dismiss ideas you have thought of in the past. We have countless stories of clients who complain that they tested a product, service or business model and it failed. Years later, a competitor launched the exact same idea with great success. What happened? The answer is that consumer behavior changed. And it is changing more rapidly every day.

Does anyone remember the Apple Newton? Likely not, but it essentially was the failed version of the smartphones we carry around today. When Apple first tried the concept, consumers weren't ready for it yet, but a short few years later they were.

What do you have in your file cabinet that could turn your business around tomorrow? A fresh look at consumer needs will answer this question.

Could insurance ever be a bought product?

Given all this, it is time to ask the question that inspired this book. Is it possible to make insurance a product that people would more actively seek? I assure you, the answer is life changing.

When you consider the trend toward consumers directing their own sale, there is reason for hope. But to get there, we need to overcome all the negatives. When it comes to insurance, people are afraid of being misled; they don't know how to figure out on their own if they have the right

coverage (or even how to determine what kind of coverage they need); and we MUST get the emotional experience of buying insurance right.

Ironically, one way to do that is to take the direct focus off insurance itself. That's what our friends at Guardian have done with a very innovative product: *The Living Balance Sheet*, which shows a person's assets and liabilities at a glance. And, obviously, once people understand how much they have to lose, they are more likely to take steps to protect what they have. And that means insurance, of course.

The nice thing about *The Living Balance Sheet*, from the consumers' perspective, is that it is not about insurance; it's about knowing and having a sense of where they are. They get to see their "status" in real time. As a result, they are ENGAGED. And they have no choice but to think of their insurance company often. It's way better than a holiday card. To me, this is one of the most insightful innovations the industry has seen, and it is NOT a price-driven one.

Yay! But has it caught on? Well, inside of Guardian, yes. But has their product taken the industry by storm and the consumer by the collar? Not yet. It's an example of the good things that can happen if you discover a need ("I wish I knew a simple way of figuring what we are worth"), create a product or service that fills that need, and communicate it effectively. And if it isn't taking the consumer by the collar, then it is just a question of how it is being commercialized.

One last word

So what do we make of all this? Well, it is clear that there are endless possibilities to alter—perhaps radically—the industry's distribution model. But if you take nothing else away from this chapter, remember

this: The absolute key to improving distribution economics is to understand the consumer really well. If you understand the consumer, you can partner with the distributor better, recruit and develop better, create better communication and better products, and present a better image to the outside world. And stop being so afraid to explore (or to let on that you are exploring) direct alternatives. The industry is far better off when we seek first to meet unmet needs.

If you don't do it, someone else will.

Things to do Monday morning:

☐ If the consumer is using salespeople for transaction validation, consider shifting the notion of sales to business development. Business development is a combination of sales, marketing and strategy that behaves in a much more consultative way. Traditional salespeople may need to be retrained or upgraded to enable them to find target markets that are looking for what they already have to offer, and for whom they can lead thought, and not be abused by the customer. Consider shifting your training budget toward some of the new skills that salespeople need in order to serve the prosumer.

☐ When you are developing a new product, add a consumer lens to the process. And take it seriously. Look at what pharma has done. They have gotten consumers to ask (their doctors) for their product.

☐ Look for ways you can embed your product into something else that consumers willingly interact with. Progressive's Flo now stars in online games, for example.

CHAPTER 7

What can we learn from "social"?

Don't confuse social with social media. Yes, social media is social, but it's only a subset of social. (Social media is covered in Chapter 11.) There are also social events, social burdens, social currency, social status, social norms and social movements. We must consider the dynamics that make social, well... social. And learn from them.

Here's the big idea: Why would you ever want to swim against the tide if you didn't have to?

There are certain societal norms, acceptable practices if you will, and we should figure out a way to take advantage of them instead of constantly fighting against them. And wanting to be part of something is about as basic as it gets when you are talking about human behavior.

The ability to be social is one of the most critical needs that people have. It is natural to want to fit in — to be part of a community. That's the reason why solitary confinement is considered such a severe punishment.

While I am not here to offer a human psychology lesson, we do want to take advantage of where people are being pulled naturally and learn from it.

Social norms

Social norms are the behaviors that people adopt in order to fit in. If your kids' friends are wearing a certain brand of jeans, rest assured your kids will want them, too. If every other 10-year-old in the neighborhood has a cell phone, your 10-year-old is also going to want one.

What are the social norms that the life insurance industry has leveraged in the past? Well, for one, the norm of a breadwinner taking care of HIS family. Yes, I said his. When the U.S. insurance industry was in one of its major growth periods, from the late 1800s and the first half of the 1900s,

the "norm" was that dad worked and mom stayed home with the kids. The message to dad was that he needed to provide for his family, and it was about more than just earning the paycheck. It was about making sure they were taken care of,even if he were not around anymore. While it does nothing for the emotional pain that would be associated with his death, it would do a lot for the financial burden.

Dial the clock forward. What are the social norms now? Two-income families. One-earner families with a woman as the earner. Two-earner families with either the man or woman as the main breadwinner. Two-earner families of the same gender. Single-person households. Single-parent households. Households containing multiple generations. Divorced families. His, mine and ours families. POSSLQs (Persons of Opposite Sex Sharing Living Quarters). All of these are "normal," yet the industry still treats the old norm like it is, well … normal.

And the answer is not creating brochures with different faces on them. That's insulting. It's about really understanding how people live their lives today, what emotions they want to feel and helping them get there.

Roughly 15 years ago, Maddock Douglas client SC Johnson tested a cleaning product designed to help busy housewives get at hard-to-reach dirt. Moms rejected the idea because they felt they already had a solution, even though it took a bit more time.

Less than five years later, the idea was one of the most successful products on the market. Why? I suspect that, in addition to being busier, moms were doing multiple jobs, playing mom, dad, employee ….

The point is that lifestyles are changing rapidly. What are we missing about how households are viewing financial decisions today under busier, higher-stress conditions?

While we have no research yet to back this, I suspect that the hectic lives that we now live won't tolerate sales pitches involving more guilt (don't you love your family?); negativity (images of crying children and funerals); and being preached to (life insurance is a miracle!). 1953 was almost a lifetime ago!

Those techniques that many of us are still using worked when people had the time to listen to them and to truly ponder the message. They also worked when the only way to find out about new products and services was through the salesperson and advertising. Now there are so many other ways to get information, and our lives have changed. (How many "traditional" couples do you know where he goes to work and she stays home with the 2.3 children?)

Since our customers' lives have changed, we need to change. How about something that makes us feel less guilty? Suze Orman, as preachy as she can be, started her rise to fame by tying the word "fabulous" to "broke" to remove the guilt associated with not having done the right thing financially in the past. She titled her book *The Money Book for the Young, Fabulous & Broke*, making it OK to be in the situation so you could do something about it.

Social status

People are very interested in where they stand compared to everyone else, whether we are talking income, elite frequent flyer status or their title at work.

What does social status look like today? Well, for many (especially younger people), it is how many friends you have on Facebook — how popular you are.

Do you remember how Facebook was started? It began as "The Face Book," and it was used to create a very cruel but intriguing champion/challenger competition among college students to see who people thought were the best looking.

Technology was able to solve the problem that people secretly wanted to know…where do I stand? Can we do it as well? *The Living Balance Sheet* I discussed in the last chapter and Mint.com could serve as great jumping off points.

Social burden

While we are constantly talking about how much of a travesty it is that we are at a 50-year low in life insurance ownership (according to 2011 LIMRA research), ask yourself this question: What is the downside of death (for the survivors)?

I know the question sounds awful, but think about it. When life insurance was an innovation, the downside of death was social burden. Widows and children on the street, selling pencils. Does that happen as much today? No. Why? Well, for one thing, there are a lot of two-income families, and one income is still going to remain. And for another, we have created safety nets, such as welfare, food stamps, Social Security benefits, in addition to various charities that are designed to help.

So what is the bigger social burden we face today? Can life insurance companies find a way to expand the definition of their business and help fix the burden of unemployment/underemployment, heath care, retirement savings and aging in place? What else is a social burden that the insurance industry can solve? (See Chapter 1.)

Social currency

This is a concept that has existed forever in some form or fashion. Social currency is the value assigned to a person in society by the others. While it is not a number per se, it is a perception of good behavior, contribution and lasting impression. People like Gandhi and Mother Theresa have the highest of social currencies. Bernie Madoff or Timothy McVeigh would have none.

What Zagats has done for restaurant ratings, eBay has done for individuals in the context of commerce with their "rate this seller." The comments and star ratings given by the people who have done business with them gives you a sense of whether or not the merchant is trustworthy. It's brilliant.

Taken a step further, Facebook has the "likes" idea that enables people to rate each other's pages, events, ideas and other contributions. The more information we all choose to put out there, or that is available for

others to put out there, the more social currency will be refined and transparent. The ultimate question of "How good am I"? can get answered.

What does social currency have to do with insurance? Well, how about reinventing the underwriting process with it?

Now that this data is becoming more readily available, could we use it in some way to enable all people to be insured, and then adjust their rates based on their social currency? Are they drunk at parties all the time? Are they texting while driving? Are they unable to hold a job?

We could also explain what it takes to be considered a good risk.

A good example of social currency "exchange" is in auto insurance. Progressive has created "Snapshot," which is a device that you put in your car and it monitors your driving in a way that can impact rates. This not only educates the customer in a positive way, but it also helps the company price more specifically and intelligently.

True story: Today, computer chips are being planted into diabetics. If their blood sugar is too low, their cars are signaled and will not start. They are then contacted immediately by a concierge service like OnStar® to see if they are OK. Once their blood sugar normalizes, their cars will start. I wonder if their insurance rates will go down? As I said before, pay attention to the intersection of behavior, technology and consumers.

Social movements

Here is one that isn't so obviously connected but could be very powerful in our learning of how to shift from push to pull. Social movements are a type of group action.

When we think about social movements, we think of things that we know are important to society, and as a result of the movement, something changes. Perhaps people quit smoking in large numbers. Maybe they stop lighting forest fires. Maybe they stop littering. For example, "Don't Mess with Texas" has become a rallying cry for a state that spells pride with a capital "P." Not many people know that it was actually a winning headline that was developed by Roy Spence and his agency GSD&M. The purpose

of the campaign was to stop Texans from littering on the sides of highways. It worked.

However, social movements are not just a way for people to naturally band together to do good for society. Sometimes social movements are created just to bring about attention and for people to be part of something bigger than themselves.

Did you know that the Occupy Wall Street movement was created by a company? Why? Because social is powerful. If you can hook into it, you will create the highest levels of pull possible.

All this social talk is to help us realize that there is untapped potential in areas we really have not explored. We keep thinking that we just need to be bigger and louder in all these messages we have been using for years. I disagree. We cannot create the future the same way we created the past. We must re-examine what has changed in social and what business we are really in. Then we must align those forces with what we want to create.

Things to do Monday morning:

- ☐ Pick up one of the coffee table books that an insurance company created for its 100th, 150th or other milestone anniversary. Look at the photos and stories and identify 10 things that have changed and 10 things that have stayed the same in the world. Then identify three things that should have changed in the business but didn't. Make initiatives out of those things.

- ☐ Watch Rachel Botsman's TED talk about collaborative consumption. http://www.youtube.com/watch?v=zpv6aGTcCl8

- ☐ Visit **occupy.com** for some insight as to how the occupy movement is organized. Stop judging them for content and look at structure.
  http://www.adbusters.org/campaigns/occupywallstreet

- ☐ Invite a social expert to your next staff meeting – not a social media expert, a social expert.

- ☐ And **(gulp)** think about how your consumers would rate you privately and publicly. Think…what kinds of understanding and behavior might make this rating better?

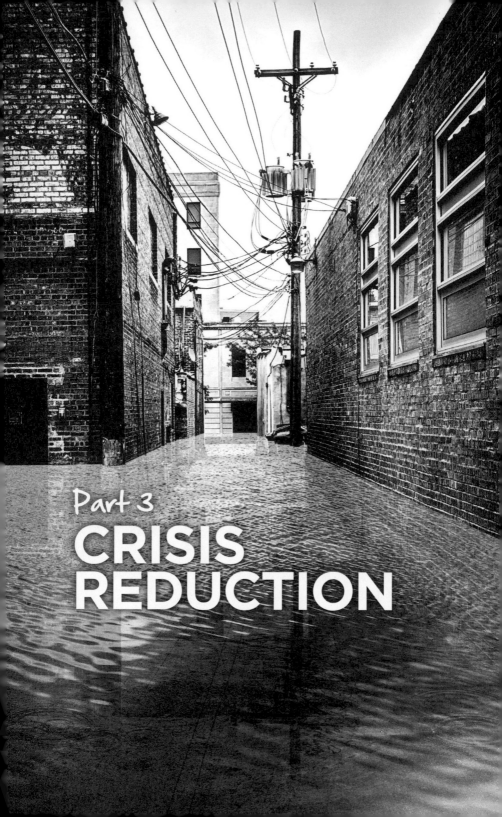

Part 3
CRISIS
REDUCTION

CHAPTER 8

Emotional rescue:
What women (and men) want

Crisis categories lack marketing nuance. Consider:
- *Every funeral parlor claims it will cater to you in time of need.*
- *Every dentist will point to his board certification*
- *There isn't an insurance company that won't say, "We're here for the long run."*

Well, duh!

People ASSUME funeral parlors will help them in moments of crisis. They ASSUME their dentist has passed industry tests. They ASSUME insurance companies will be here tomorrow. Those aren't benefits or differentiators. They are givens, and they are not going to resonate with customers.

Truly understanding the emotions behind the behaviors of our customers is key to creating both effective messages and successful marketing.

Often, "uninterested" is the label we give to those who are not responding to our messages when it turns out the reality is that these people are truly interested in learning more about our offerings, if only we understood their concerns.

For example, many people, particularly women, are embarrassed to show a financial advisor, mechanic or doctor how little they know about their own "equipment." But they will rarely admit that. Rather, they will respond to our message or sales pitch with "I'm too busy right now to think about it," or even "I don't like you." The marketer's **perception and the reality** don't necessarily match.

Here's a quick example from another industry: About five years ago, we did some work for an engine additive company that created products for outdoor power equipment like lawn mowers. The new product that we launched hinged directly on the facts that:

1. Women were now cutting a heck of a lot of lawns, and
2. Fixing power equipment has become a lost art. Many dads were too busy in the last generation to teach their kids how to fix things.

Nobody told us these things. We actually learned both by observing households doing lawn care activities and trying to start equipment. The point: Researchers understand the old axiom — actions speak louder than words.

But we don't always observe correctly, and then we compound the problem. Because insurance has a "later benefit" (i.e., people write the check today but don't receive anything — other than peace of mind — until later), there can be a natural tendency among potential customers to put off the purchase.

Our usual response to that? We try to "guilt" them into buying. For example, we'll ask, "Don't you love your family?" or "What do you think would happen to your family if you didn't come home tonight?" This is a common tactic used in the sales process of insurance products.

The reality is, while many of our potential customers do love their families, they also are feeling other emotions that they are not proud of or are willing to express outwardly. These may include their own guilt, anger, resentment and other things they do not think they have permission to feel toward their loved ones. They then may transfer some of those feelings onto the person trying to sell them something.

So is guilting them into action the right approach to take? Until we truly know our customers, it is impossible to answer the question. What we have proven time and time again is making assumptions about them is the wrong way to go.

Take the recent credit crisis.

The role that federal policymakers and those in the financial services industry have been well documented. We were enticing consumers with the prospect of "giving them the house that they and their families deserve" by offering $500,000, no-money-down mortgages to 20-somethings making less than $100,000 a year. What were we thinking?

But depending on who you ask, you will get different answers about which consumers' emotionally driven attitudes and behaviors helped drive the credit crisis.

Take a look at the following table for some characteristics of different generations. Could we point to any of these behaviors as driving the credit crisis? Was it the boomers and their "I want it now" ways? Was it Gen Y and their lack of understanding about how money works?

PERSONAL AND LIFESTYLE CHARACTERISTICS BY GENERATION

	Veterans (1922 – 1945)	Baby Boomers (1946 – 1964)	Generation X (1965 – 1980)	Generation Y (1981 – 2000)
Core Values	• Respect for authority • Conformers • Discipline	• Optimism • Involvement	• Skepticism • Fun • Informality	• Realism • Confidence • Extreme fun • Social
Family	• Traditional • Nuclear	• Disintegrating	• Latch-key kids	• Merged families
Education	• A dream	• A birthright	• A way to get there	• An incredible expense
Communication Media	• Rotary phones • One-on-one • Write a memo	• Touch-tone phones • Call me anytime	• Cell phones • Call me only at work	• Internet • Picture phones • Email
Dealing with Money	• Put it away • Pay cash	• Buy now, pay later	• Cautious • Conservative • Save, save, save	• Earn to spend

Source: FDU Magazine Winter/Spring 2005 "Mixing and Managing Four Generations of Employees," Greg Hammill

The truth is, you will find people who use and abuse credit differently no matter what generation they are in. I know Gen Yers who are great savers, veterans who are living on credit and baby boomers who are proud to be seen driving used cars. But the bottom line is that too many people, regardless of segment, were/are confusing their credit lines with cash.

Plastic beats brick/stucco/split-levels

A recent study by Iconowatch, a global research firm, showed that there is a new, emerging hierarchy that more than 30 percent of Americans are following when they pay their bills. They are paying credit cards first, mortgages second. That would make some people's hair (regardless of the color or density) stand on end, but for others, it is the way to keep and sustain available funds for emergencies in an economy where unemployment is high and credit is at a premium.

Not surprisingly, the heaviest users of this technique to keep credit scores up—and amazingly it does—are the ones with the lowest scores. And they are not always generationally determined.

What opportunity does all this present for an innovator? Well, first, it is important to jump ahead of your competition who is still probably trying to use generational distinctions to determine financial behaviors. Perhaps you are assuming that Gen Y is not a market for investing because either they don't have enough money or they can't get out of their own way. Perhaps you believe that people over 65 aren't in need of better management of their debts and cash flow. Perhaps you think that people without kids don't want life insurance. But how will you know for sure?

You have to get to know your customers. The right kind of qualitative and quantitative research will help you understand their needs, desires and tensions through deep insight. (See Chapters 11 and 15.) And the insights you are looking for are extremely specific. They are not just about what people like or dislike, they are about finding an unsolved need that, if solved, will make them buy something. If you develop the right insights, they may just turn your original assumptions on their head.

I am not kidding. Think about your favorite sports team.

Play ball!

Imagine you're the one in the room with the honor of being the least knowledgeable about football, basketball, hockey or baseball. You'd have no business writing anything sports related. Luckily, *ESPN The Magazine*

recently asked *Maddock Douglas* to figure out why people support their favorite teams. The results made us do "the wave."

ESPN wanted to know what created fan loyalty, and what we found out by surveying a representative of people was fascinating.

Sports teams run on statistics. Players are signed, promoted, rewarded or released based on how well they perform against an agreed-upon set of detailed metrics. Yet when it comes to figuring out the best way to attract and keep fans, it's a whole other matter. These same teams are, for the most part, relying on either outdated research approaches or "gut feel" to determine what fans want. **(Hmmm, sounds like our industry, doesn't it?)** And not surprisingly, they are swinging and missing. Want proof? Consider some of Maddock Douglas' findings:

- Every sports executive says the number one thing fans want is a winning team. Fans rank it eleventh when asked why they show up at a game.
- What the paying customers want most is a "fan-friendly" environment, right? Nope. Fans rank it sixth in importance.
- Teams worry that their ticket prices are too high. Fans say cost ranks seventh when they are deciding whether or not to attend a game.

This discrepancy between what sports executives believe and what is actually going on in the marketplace reveals that most have failed to take notice of two related and depressing facts:

- Few sports teams recognize the power of their brand/customer relationship.
- Most fail to leverage the unshakable fan loyalty simply because they have not taken the time to figure out what fans truly care about.

Again, I don't know the first thing about sports, but I do know something about our industry, and I think we are just as out of touch with our customers as owners of professional sports teams are.

Digging a little deeper in the study, I found some interesting facts that also seem to have parallels for us.

For example, fans:

- Placed more value on the effort and commitment that the teams made around winning than whether or not they were actually winning
- Cared more about having strong leaders as coaches than they did about a team's willingness to pay a high price for good players
- Were more interested in whether or not players acted professionally on and off the field than they did about anything related to price (tickets, parking, concessions, etc.)
- Cared more about whether or not the players treated their fans with respect than they did about actually having access to those players

The big "aha!" is that fans want to like their teams, respect them and be respected more than they need games to be won – or prices to be lower.

FAN FAVORITE: USAA

USAA seems to have lots of fans. Maybe it is because they are focused on fewer segments. Since they focus on military families, they naturally have the advantage of more deeply understanding their customers. They can communicate more intimately and develop products and services just for them. This is exactly why many consumer packaged goods companies organize their product lines by segments—so their brand managers can leverage a deeper understanding of their consumers.

How long before other insurance companies take advantage of this same idea?

So what's the application to financial services companies? Well, first, it may be valuable to create "fandom" within your customer base. Perhaps there should be more thought and innovation put around making customers feel respected versus products that will squeeze out a little more return for them – or lowering prices.

Here are a few hunches that you may want to consider:

1. If your customers like you, would they be more likely to pay more for your products and services?

2. If your customers feel respected, would they be less likely to engage in a lawsuit when investment performance is not there? (Hint: The number one factor that keeps people from suing their physicians in the case of malpractice? They like their doctor.)

3. If your customers respect you, would they be more likely to tolerate a mistake and not immediately go elsewhere?

4. If your customers like you, respect you and feel respected, would they paint their bodies in your logo color and hold up a foam finger in your honor? (I was just checking to see if you read this far.)

Things to do Monday morning:

☐ De-guilt your marketing messages and training messages. If you don't think you have any, look harder. Do you have anything that is designed to imply that someone is doing the wrong thing by his or her family? Do your reps do this as a matter of routine? It is not working.

☐ Unassume your market segments by their demographics and generational considerations. Yes, Gen Y is befuddling, but it is not a monolithic group by any stretch.

☐ Rethink the assumptions you are making about customer loyalty, price features, etc. Try out some new things that make people feel respected, loved and important.

☐ Revisit the question: "What business are we really in?" and add this thought: "What business could we be in?"

CHAPTER 9

The Reverse Elevator™ test: Transparency redefined

There is a very big difference between being heard and being understood. If there is one area that a company in a crisis category could own, it is the idea of being understood.

Here I am going to talk about making sure you are communicating effectively.

The products and service models we offer in the insurance and financial industries are riddled with complexity. And with that complexity comes potential misunderstanding.

Think back to the financial meltdown of 2008 and the Congressional hearings that followed. A focus of one of the hearings was on how synthetic collateral debt obligations (CDOs) work. I wasn't sure myself, so I went to an online tutorial that gave a "simplified" diagram and narrative. It took them about eight minutes to provide the simple explanation.

As I watched Goldman Sachs' CEO talk to a Senate panel a couple of days later, I was struck by how complex and confusing his answers sounded when he was asked about many issues, including the operation of synthetic CDOs. He started by explaining a CDO, then he was interrupted by a senator, requesting the answer to what a synthetic CDO was, and he argued that he needed to explain a CDO before he could explain a synthetic CDO. Needless to say, it was awfully difficult to explain how buying a synthetic CDO was in the best interests of investors when the issuer (Goldman Sachs in this case) would make the most money if the purchasers lost theirs.

The fact that Goldman Sachs was betting against the market was an easy sound byte. The part about how the investment was supposed to work was not.

That is not to say that all complex products are bad for the consumer. Our smartphones are incredibly complicated, and you would be hard pressed to find someone willing to live without one.

But complex products can be confusing. And that frequently creates an opening for innovation. If people don't understand how they work, someone who can explain it has a huge edge.

This always seemed self-evident to me. Yet we seem to go out of our way to confuse things when we talk about products and services. Maddock Douglas' research shows that many of the words we use are either not understood or associated with something unrelated, particularly with many potential consumers, especially Gen Y. (More on this in Chapter 10.)

IT CAN BE DONE

To everyone who says, "Our industry is so regulated that innovation is close to impossible," I say, "Poppycock." Fidelity and Vanguard have made 401(k)s relatively simple, and the investment industry is just as heavily regulated (if not more) as insurance.

The automobile insurance industry is also about as heavily regulated as life insurance, yet they have come up with ways to innovate and even have fun. Have you seen the Progressive ads featuring Flo?

You can love the character or hate her, but there is no doubt that she has been effective in:

A.   Communicating that when you go to Progressive's website, you can compare its prices against the competition, even if Progressive is more expensive (people love this kind of transparency)

B.   Explaining that Progressive will let you, in essence, write your own insurance policy, with you picking just the coverage you want

C.   Saving you money if you give Progressive a bit of information about the way you drive

If a car insurer can do this sort of thing, we can too.

So products, services and ways of doing business can be laden with confusion. Clearing that smoke is an opportunity to gain attention and more business. Granted, changing our way of communicating isn't that easy in a highly regulated industry.

But it represents a real opportunity for anyone who can say it differently—and convince the regulators that it is in the consumers' best interest to do so.

What are the best ways to find these disconnects and turn them into opportunities? There are three places to look:

1. **Lean into the misunderstanding.** Look for the places where people go "huh?" when you are explaining what you have to sell. Look also for the emotions that go along with that reaction. Do they feel stupid or ashamed that they don't understand? Do they get angry with the communicator? Are they just truly indifferent? Do they really want to know the answer? For example, let's suppose a financial advisor is launching into a long spiel about the risks of an insurance or investment product, and the client's eyes glaze over during a discussion of dollar cost averaging. The consumer's response could mean anything from annoyance to confusion to total indifference and wishing the advisor would just finish already. So the communicator should flat out ask her client why his eyes are glazing and change her approach accordingly.

2. **Find what IS understood.** Research here is important. Find out what customers say they understand, even if they are wrong. If people are describing your product or service incorrectly, it is a sign you don't have the right positioning. If they are describing it correctly, it is valuable in helping your pitch sound like English. Look for the benefits that they took away. Listen to what words they use to describe it. Pay attention to what makes the "light bulb" go on. A great test is to ask your grandmothers, grandfathers (unless you have grandparents in finance) or children under 10 if they understand what you are talking about. It isn't patronizing. It's a way to make sure your message is getting through.

3. **Build a bridge.** This is where you create a new way to communicate the product in a way that people "get it." Make sure it is a bridge to the purpose for the product and not to something that is just easy to latch onto. For example, if it's an investment

offering, your bridge should be about the philosophy, management and time horizon, not about the past returns. Otherwise, confusion is bound to get even worse when the product does not perform as hoped. More clients sue their financial advisors in down markets than up, regardless of how well they understand what they bought. In 2009, the auto industry was in terrible shape. The recession was in full tilt and nobody was buying cars. Then someone at Hyundai had a brilliant idea: If you lose your job, we'll let you walk away from your car loan. This simple idea literally jump-started sales for the company — and then eventually copied by competitors — the entire industry. This idea started with a simple insight: Consumers wanted to buy but were afraid of losing their jobs. Then, behind the scenes, marketing got together with finance and got them to say, "Sure, we could insure that idea." But nobody said anything about insurance in the ad. Instead, they spoke directly to the unmet need — and biggest fear — of the consumer. Brilliant ideas like this are readily available for any insurance company that works to uncover unmet consumer needs.

4. **Use technology to make it easier.** Let's face it — much of your budget for IT is being used to do stuff with old technology. I know, it is the nature of the legacy system beast. However, some of your budget should be earmarked for allowing the newest of the new technologies to help make understanding the products and how they work a lot easier. Some of these technologies are not super expensive and don't have to link in to other systems to get the job done. Whiteboard animations — think the UPS TV ad where the long-haired guy is drawing — are a great example of a simple idea that is made interesting and aids people's understanding by leveraging technology.

What I am talking about here is no easy task; however, no great opportunity ever is. Having a good process for discovering the insight, developing and testing the ideas, and communicating them is key. (Please see the three circles of innovation in Chapter 1.)

Reflections of transparency

Illiquidity insolvencies, Ponzi schemes, financial institutions betting against investors, complicated derivatives, lawsuits from consumers who feel duped....

Sounds like a bad dream. But for some forward-thinking leaders and savvy innovators, this is clearly an opportunity to differentiate, create customer satisfaction and more loyalty, and, more important, invent what's next.

There is absolutely no doubt that government, investors, the public in general – and, yes, some corporations and industry executives – are thinking a great deal about transparency, which I define as "clearly and effectively communicating how what we are selling works, and what's in it for every party involved."

Transparency seems to be the obvious answer for giving our customers what they need to make informed decisions. But the consumer must really understand.

Transparency: What it is and what it isn't

It is very important to make the distinction between transparency and its mousy counterpart called disclosure. The difference between the two is intent.

If the intention of the "offerer" is primarily to comply with rules, laws and regulations, or to answer questions that investors have, that is likely disclosure. Whether it is "full" or not makes little difference in its effectiveness. Disclosure is often linear, piecemeal, word polluted and/or complicated to find – and understand. For example, some disclosures are all strung together in one section and easy to skip. I am talking about things like: *Not a deposit. Not FDIC or NCUSIF insured. Not guaranteed by the institution. Not insured by any federal government agency. May lose value.*

But it often is a requirement. And that is how most companies treat it – like going to the dentist or getting a colonoscopy. They turn the problem over to the lawyers who create the language like you saw above,

and investors promptly ignore it and just do what an advisor or a friend tells them to do.

Transparency, on the other hand, is intended to help the "offeree" make the right decision for them. Transparency paints a picture. It tells a story. It instills a feeling. This may require a different kind of thinking to accomplish; however, it also offers significant opportunities for those who know how to provide it, and for those companies that leverage it.

Let's use an example from a parallel industry to prove the point. Which firm would you rather deal with? One who defines a leverage buy-out this way?

> *Leverage is the use of a target company's asset value to finance the debt incurred in acquiring said company. Typically, the acquirer uses a significant amount of borrowed money – bonds, loans or other debt obligations – to meet the cost of the acquisition. Often, the assets of the company being acquired are used as collateral for the loans in addition to the assets of the acquiring company.*

Or this one?

> *Did you ever buy a house or know someone who did? Well, a leverage buyout works the same way. You make a downpayment with your money and borrow the rest. And just like when you buy a house, the company you acquire is used as collateral.*

More than 10 years ago, Maddock Douglas was hired by AT&T to remake their billing experience. Why? Because their bill was so confusing it was making their customers angry, among other things. It's hard to cross-sell to angry and confused customers. Want to see how transparent you are? Take one of your billing statements into a focus group and buckle up. It's going to be a rough ride.

Who should set the example for transparency?

Recently, regulatory bodies such as the SEC, the FDIC and state insurance departments have issued reports or proposals to require transparency in response to the outcry from the public, post financial institution bailouts, failures, market volatility and Madoff's $65 billion fraud. Some of these ideas include requiring every bank to develop a "living will" (a contingency plan for failure) and demanding disclosure of commissions paid on insurance products. But is the government the place where you gain transparency, or just more disclosure?

Sounds like more disclosure. And while it may be useful to some, it can't prevent the next big issue from happening because it is all rear view mirror stuff.

It would be better if the companies and institutions themselves set the example by proactively looking for ways to have investors see the strategies, how value is created and how money is made. Not only would investors become better educated, but they would be more inclined to trust the institutions if they understand how and why they do what they do. Imagine the brand loyalty to a company whose customers can actually understand what they are paying in fees, but also why it is fair.

"You know it when you see it"

PricewaterhouseCoopers put together a paper a couple of years ago on what comprises transparent financial reporting and how you can make the right information more accessible and effective.

In a perfect world, PwC argued that you would know you have transparency when the consumer can do the following three things:

1. Explain CORRECTLY to someone else how the investment works
2. Know the circumstances under which the desired results would not be achieved (i.e., insolvencies, poor market performance, subpar management performance, etc.)
3. Understand who makes money in the transaction, how they make money, and when they are likely to make the most or least

money (i.e., Do they make more when you make more? Or do they make the same when you make less, etc.?)

A company that is committed to transparency would want everyone who works for them to be committed to making sure the customer truly understands how its products work and would want a way to measure that they are achieving that goal. Imagine that kind of trust as a differentiator?

Who is doing that?

There are a number of new innovations that are springing up to address transparency in different ways. For example, some companies are now "showing their work." JP Morgan has introduced an iPad app that gives customers access to research and economic indicators used by the pros in order to make investing decisions. E-trade has created online trading apps to put similar professional strength information in the hands of the ordinary investor. In addition to giving clients more tools to use so they can take more control over their investment if they wish, it shows customers how these firms make decisions that will effect their clients' investments.

In the 401(k) world, Putnam recently announced an innovation in their fee transparency initiatives to help plan sponsors and participants understand the "big picture" in fee structures. Literally, they are using pictures, not just required words, to help people really understand what kinds of fees they are incurring and for what. This is a great step in the right direction. It shows intent of understanding, not just compliance.

All this is good, but I think we can do more. How about a customer survey that "tests" to make sure people understand what they are buying? How about an entertaining and engaging way to fill the gap in knowledge if it is found to be too wide? Like if they are failing on the terminology, why not create a little musical video that embeds the words into their heads like they do on Sesame Street? How about a way for the company to publish its results and progress in this area like it would its financial results? Perhaps an objective third party could rate how well they are doing à la the Good Housekeeping Seal of Approval or a J.D. Power's rating?

While transparency is still a "young" concept in the financial world, it offers a lot of opportunity for differentiation and innovation among companies that have the right intentions and are also willing to lead change. And those innovations can take place in many parts of the business – new products/services and new business/communication models.

This requires specific research. It also requires listening to the language our customers use to describe what we sell, and using their language – and not our jargon – to describe our offerings.

How will you know you are successful? This is where the Reverse Elevator™ speech test comes in.

As you know, an "elevator speech" is a 30-second explanation you give that describes what you do/have and why it is beneficial. It is called an elevator speech because presumably you could give it in an elevator to someone just going a few floors along with you.

The Reverse Elevator™ speech, a term I coined, is one that the person gives about you after you leave the elevator. In other words, it's what he/she has taken away from your message.

You know your message is received when:

A.   The Reverse Elevator™ speech is a close match to the elevator speech.

B.   There is positive emotion associated with the interaction.

Where can we start? Unclaimed touchpoints

I have talked throughout about the importance of emotional engagement. And not surprisingly when I do, thoughts typically turn to what we can do to increase the level of involvement when it comes to our commercial messages, brochures and maybe the sales force itself.

All that is good, but there are so many more areas we could improve. For example, routine correspondence (bills, letters, updates, statements...). These tend to be very ordinary and they don't – to be blunt – create a great client experience, as when I was talking about Maddock Douglas' work with AT&T. Efforts have been made to make them more understandable, but would anyone consider making them entertaining – or

thought provoking – versus just stating the facts? For example, would anyone ever consider sending company updates in the form of a funny and entertaining YouTube video? Would they consider a talking bill? Perhaps a letter with pictures or graphics on it? Or even better, eliminating some of the needless things that clients throw out anyway, like privacy statements, or prospectuses, or anything else printed on that really thin, cheap newsy kind of paper? (To make the lawyers happy, we could probably post everything legally required on our website.)

And imagine if the content of the required disclosures could be incorporated into the body of the message in a way that people read it, understood it, remembered it and/or even liked it? For example, instead of saying, "Past performance is no indication of future results," why not say, "Here's how this fund did over the last few years; market rates vary, so next year the return could be higher or lower. To learn more about how to be a smarter investor, investing in general and the stock market in particular, click here."

In other words, make this the headline, not the footnote, and give people lots and lots and lots of objective information so that they can become a smarter consumer!

There is no end to the possibilities of what you can do to differentiate yourself. Think about computer error messages. Suppose these were funny versus onerous or making one feel like they just made a stupid mistake that the nerd patrol is now laughing at? If "fatal error" all of a sudden turned into "please excuse my chip fart..." more customers would stop, smile and perhaps even tell someone about it.

Particularly in our industry, companies that wish to differentiate themselves from the pack have a significant opportunity. If today's consumers identify with your company because they fully understand what you have to sell and you empowered them to make good financial decisions, you will have laid claim to an area of white space that nobody owns yet. And if their experience is more engaging and positive in the process, it will be easier to attract buyers.

Things to do Monday morning:

☐ Find the real disconnects in your consumers' understanding. Look for the disconnects that are pervasive, and consider them your biggest opportunities.

☐ Know the difference between disclosing information and being transparent.

☐ Take ownership for "living" transparency and not just saying it. Check your routine correspondence, disclosures, error messages and other places where "moments" matter.

☐ Use the Reverse Elevator™ speech to test yourself.

☐ Show me an insurance company that doesn't take itself too seriously and I'll show you a competitive advantage.

CHAPTER 10

U talking 2 me?
The role of language in
complex categories

No one will be shocked if I say that "echo boomers" (aka Gen Y, those people now in their 20s and early 30s who are the children of the original baby boomers) are not a primary target for the financial services industry. **(Heck, this segment is basically ignored.)**

When asked why (or Y not?), industry executives say such things as "well, they don't have any money," or "their finances are a mess," or "they just don't think about their own mortality enough to take any action."

Potentially valid reasons all. But industry sales are flat, the percentage of households owning life insurance has fallen to its lowest levels in 50 years according to LIMRA, and the regulatory environment is putting the whole industry under attack. With all of that going on, one must wonder where growth is going to come from, and once again, we are back to looking at Gen Y as an opportunity.

As a Gen Xer (i.e., those who were born between the baby boomers and Gen Y), I have observed how boomers have raised their kids. And while I am not judging, there are certain things that are hard to ignore. For example, boomers have problems letting go. They have been called "helicopter parents" because of their tendency to hover near — by becoming involved in every part of their kids' lives.

The psychology behind that (Is it because their own parents were distant? Is it because they don't trust their kids?) is not for us to figure out. But it is there, and it raises a couple of interesting ideas for us to explore.

Is there a way to reach Gen Y through their parents? Gen Y, even though they are mostly of "adult" age, rely heavily on their parents for advice and tend to live in an extended state of adolescence. If you believe that, then parents should be considered a key center of influence to Gen Y.

The other thought is a negative one. Could it be that the real reason why insurance companies – being run primarily by baby boomers these days – do not take Gen Y seriously is because, as I said before, they look at them like their own children, or even grandchildren, and not as their future customers? That is troubling, if true.

The fact is, eventually Gen Y will grow up and recognize they have long-term financial needs and someone will fill them. But who? How? And with what?

But before you start trying to think of ways to satisfy their needs, there is something you need to know....

They are just not that into you.

Sigh. (Junior high feelings come rushing back: anger, sadness, desire for a new wardrobe or haircut, perhaps....)

But the ironic part is that they are into the things the insurance industry believes in. They are very community and charity minded; they want to help the greater good. They also have high aspirations for their own lives and careers. They want to run their own businesses, start their own causes, have families. And what you provide, namely protection against risks that could screw up their lives and the lives of others, should be a product they want. So what gives?

That's simple. They don't have a clue what you are talking about.

How did this gap happen?

The language of the insurance industry was created in another era – a couple of centuries ago to be exact. In the 1800s, public social programs didn't exist and the insurance industry filled the void, protecting people from catastrophe. Not surprisingly, the language that insurance companies used described what the insurance companies focused on and the role they were fulfilling, not what individuals needed.

Take the word "policy." What is a policy? It is the company's set of structures and rules for how it pays out money. It isn't a product that is for the consumer. It's about what the company will "allow."

How about "agent"? An agent, in insurance-speak, means someone who represents the company – not someone who represents the customer.

Waiver? The word means that the company foregoes its right to something. It is saying that if you purchase this benefit, the company will waive its right to collect premiums.

Who's the center of the universe there?

Let's look at one more example: Claim. Back then it was about claiming that you had a right to the proceeds and being given the opportunity to prove it. It reminds me of Dorothy and the Wizard of Oz. She lands in this crazy place; has to walk for miles; meets all kinds of nutty ridiculous people/animals; risks her life to get the ruby slippers; and then has to prove that she is worthy of going home? *(That's probably where the term "Gee, Wiz" comes from....)*

C'mon. Do you have kids in their 20s or early 30s *(or know any)*? How would they respond to a structure that was all about the company and not about them? How is it that other industries are morphing and changing to consumer-centricity while we are struggling along with a "build it and *(hopefully)* they shall come" model? Industries like banking, travel and music have become much more consumer-centric in their business models. Heck, even the IRS has become more customer-centric by allowing electronic filings and direct deposit of refunds!

Years ago, the U.S. Postal Service (USPS) was the only way to get a letter or package from point A to point B. Like any other business or organization that has a monopoly, the USPS predictably did not listen to the changing needs of its consumers. Enter UPS and FedEx. Today, the U.S. Postal Service – an entity that started in business 132 years before UPS and one that has the backing of the U.S. Government – is losing billions of dollar and is scrambling to stay relevant and alive, despite having nearly a two century head start on FedEx. Any organization that loses track of the needs of its END consumers is doomed to fail eventually.

That's why we need to pay attention to Gen Y. And if boomers are the "me generation," the echo boomers (Gen Y) wouldn't be "Mini Me," they would be "Maxi Me."

That's a contorted way of saying they feel even more entitled to be catered to by the brands they engage with than their boomer parents do. And clearly we are failing to respond to their needs because the general public, especially Gen Y, does not understand insurance very well at all.

I'd like to teach the (insurance) world to sing

A recent study by Maddock Douglas proves that the issue of the consumers' lack of understanding of insurance, and their negative emotions about the things they do understand, is pervasive. However, both of these things represent a significant opportunity for companies that are willing to step up and change the language of the insurance industry.

The study tested some commonly used words and concepts and asked respondents to associate the words and/or define them. While the

group as a whole was not really familiar with insurance terminology, it was worse within Gen Y than with boomers. This makes sense when you think about it. The further a generation gets away from the roots of the business, the less relevant that business will seem – unless, of course, the language and offerings keep up with the times.

Let's look at a few key examples where the language has *not* kept up.

Protection. This is a word used in most insurance marketing materials. And it is good that half of respondents think about it as security. But why do, as the following chart shows, more people associate it with birth control than insurance?

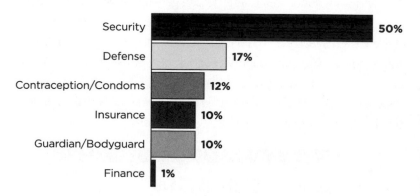

How about that **policy**? While many do associate the word with insurance, you can see a marked difference between how boomers think about the word and their kids do.

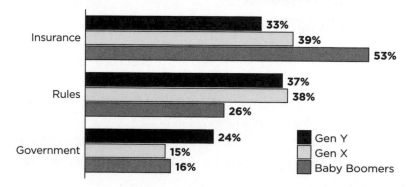

What about **disability** insurance? The word disability is more often associated with handicaps, yet we use it to describe coverage for people who are injured or who become unable to work.

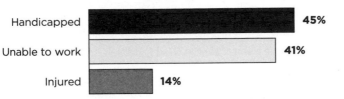

And what about financial services in general? Most insurance companies have entered into the retirement space in one way or another. While it seems reasonable and responsible to help younger people save wisely, how do younger people feel about the word "retirement?" As you can see, boomers have a more favorable view of the word, and younger generations associate it more with old age than they do with the freedom that boomers associate it with.

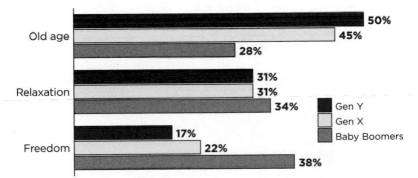

It is important to understand that one size does not fit all here. If you unilaterally changed your communication strategy to appeal to Gen Y, you'd confuse the boomers. The point is that a "Who" business creates specific language to be evocative to EACH of their consumer segments. A "What" business often uses language that is familiar and comfortable to the people selling the product but, in the process, ignores and confuses their customers.

Emotional rescue

The bottom line is that the positive emotions the industry is trying to create through feelings of satisfaction, confidence and relief are being crowded out by negative ones.

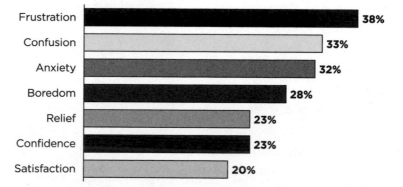

When we asked respondents who they thought benefited the most from insurance, the providers themselves came out #1 and consumers #5. Yikes!

Who benefits from insurance?

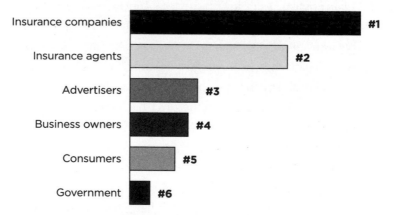

However, perception is reality, and it is something to contend with. It is a signal that the relevance and value are not being seen as they could be or should be.

So what's the good news?

If it's white space and you know it clap your hands!

When we asked consumers who they thought needed to be responsible for making them understand insurance, they accepted a lot of the responsibility! So they want to know about it, and they probably know that what we offer is important.

What does that mean for forward-thinking insurance companies? It means "white space." That is, the opportunity to own something that no competitor does. When it comes to language, nobody is really doing well…yet. Here are a few areas at which to look:

34%
Insurance company
is responsible

49%
Insurance company
and consumers are
equally responsible

16%
Consumers are
responsible

1. **Plain English.** Yes, plain English is legal. Your explanations and disclosures do not need to read like a lawyer wrote it in order to comply with various regulations. Do most people understand what plain English means? It's not just the avoidance of big complex words, but also a conversational style that people would use every day. A simple example from the AT&T bill: We changed the language "balance due" to "what you owe." Why? Because we heard many frustrated customers say, "I just want to know what I owe."

2. **Style.** Can you set up your correspondence to be read without reading? Bold headlines that complete a thought, not just tease it. Callout boxes. Bulleted lists. Anything that can respect the reader's time and energy commitment to getting through the document. How many of us go to McDonald's and order the #2, as opposed to asking for a quarter pounder, fries and a soft drink (which, of course, makes up the #2)? Look around and you'll see

almost every industry has found ways to quickly communicate products and services to a population that is growing less patient with companies that don't know what they want well enough to be succinct.

3. **Tone.** Is it engaging? Maybe funny? Maybe it takes the reader by surprise? Insurance companies are scared to death of doing this because financial topics are considered serious. However, day-to-day life is something people want to feel lighthearted about, and your finances and risk management, if we are doing our job right, should become a part of our everyday life.

Are you still complaining about your legal department? Stop asking them for approval and start partnering with them. If you allow them to write for consumers directly without giving them the insight, that's unfair to everyone. They need to be at the table, solving these problems with you.

We took on an innovation assignment for an insurance client who complained that legal never approved of anything. We involved key stake-holders from legal in the project, and not only did we have a new product in market in fewer than six months, but the winning idea was directly tied to an insight that the lawyers brought to the table.

Things to do Monday morning:

☐ Identify the words and phrases that you use all the time in your communications and re-examine them for how they might sound to a younger person.

☐ Get a copy of the Maddock Douglas insurance language study and look at the section on product names. Consider renaming some to align with what consumers find more relevant. http://language.soldnotbought.com

☐ When you are coming up with new communications, consider the tone in which they are written and determine if they sound more like your parent's or grandparent's voice, or your kid's voice. Opt for your kid's.

CHAPTER 11

Avoiding the land shark: Social media dynamics and thought leadership (or get out of my Facebook!)

We must employ social media very differently in crisis categories like insurance. The approach to use boils down to this: social first, media second.

The people who use social networks are not looking for your commercial, and when they see one from you, it infuriates them. Not only do they want to avoid your product to begin with, you are now invading their space. Whatever (tiny) goodwill they felt toward you is gone.

Many companies believe they are satisfying their social media line item in their marketing plans by creating a Facebook, Twitter or LinkedIn account for their brand. But if you take a look, you'll see that followership is very low. Why? Because the people who use social networks – and remember, they are our customers and potential customers – see such things as a randomly placed tweet or post about an insurance product as noise, nuisance and spam.

I have seen more than one insurance agent or insurance company attempt to use social media as a pulpit for preaching about what they do and how it helps people. And, of course, they do help people, but that message is not going to be received well by people who are in the midst of a search for their high school sweetheart, or looking for the perfect place to go on vacation.

Having the wrong presence on social media can actually be worse than having no presence at all.

The way to handle social media is through a well-developed thought leadership platform that isolates an ownable area of expertise and builds a brand around that. And that brand may not be your company's name, by the way.

As I listen to and observe the challenges, approaches and results of social media in the insurance industry, I cannot help but think about the original cast of *Saturday Night Live* and their "Land Shark" skit. It evolved out of the hype from the movie "Jaws." In the *SNL* version, a land shark **(i.e., one that literally could walk on land)** tried various ruses — he would pretend to be a florist or be delivering a candy gram — to get into the homes so he could devour the people inside.

This is the way that some insurance companies are approaching social media. They put a Facebook page out there pretending they want to "make friends," but what they are really looking to do is sell products. And it's just as obvious as that land shark was. People see through it, and all of a sudden we have given those potential customers another reason not to do business with us.

Multilevel marketing firms use this type of social strategy to drive business. Your "friends" ask you over to their home for what you think is a social gathering, only to be back door pitched on a skin care, weight loss or vitamin product. Some insurance organizations have even dabbled with this strategy. Yikes, right? Nobody likes it when it happens to them face-to-face, and they don't like it any better when it happens to them online.

Want proof? Look at the number of "likes" the pages receive from Facebook users who rate the offering. Some of the major insurance brands have fewer than 10,000 likes. By way of comparison, Target has more than 17 million likes, Lady Gaga has more than 53 million and Facebook itself more than 70 million.

By contrast, Farmers Insurance has more than 2 million likes. What are they doing right? They are talking about socially related items of interest to get people engaged. They are discussing NASCAR, not products or brand. They FIRST discuss things their potential customers are interested in. They are not trying to move product initially.

This is an important point. Of course, any marketing expenditure you make should produce more in the way of income than you spend. So, yes, it is OK to mention your product and how it can help people. But that pitch — especially when it appears on social media — can only be effective

if you first prove yourself to be someone who can be genuinely helpful or funny or entertaining to the people on the social media site.

Get it? Farmers does this well. As does Progressive, which I will discuss a bit later. Check out their social media tone on Facebook. Also, for a different tone but still very social, check out Aviva and its Youmanity Program, a way of engaging communities to give back.

Social first, media second

Let's expand on what I just talked about. While social media is a powerful force in reaching large numbers of people, we must remember that users are not going to it to find products and services. They are on these sites to make connections, stay in touch and network with people who they choose.

The biggest mistake that I see in the application of social media in the insurance industry is that we are taking the messages used in traditional advertising media (like TV and print) and placing them on the social media "channels" like LinkedIn, Facebook and Twitter. Done this way, this will — at best — result in just a small number of followers and fans, and at worst, annoy the users to the point where even the relevant messages will be ignored and the brand could be damaged. Why? Because once people see a company pushing product through social media, they push the eject button and it takes a long while for them to trust that they should give anything else from that company a second look.

Innovation in communication

Innovative marketers need to remember that social media works because of "who and what." *Who* is saying it and *what* they are saying. "Who" needs to be, as I said, someone of trust and expertise in an area. "What" is the resonating message that makes sense in a sound bite or two.

If we are going to execute against this approach, we will have to change our messaging. When we get around to talking about our products — and again, this should NOT be the thing we lead with to engage our customers and potential customers on social media — instead of talk-

ing about what our products do, we will need to explain how it helps the person on social media. And we will need to have that message delivered by someone who is both genuine and credible.

The innovation here lays in "breaking open" the traditional message into small, relevant pieces and using them to pull interest versus push product. For example, instead of saying, "We pay claims faster than any company," why not say, "Don't you hate it when you have to wait forever to get the money after a fender bender?" This pulls. It's emotional. It's relatable.

What is necessary for better results?

So how do you do what I just talked about?

1. Give your Facebook, LinkedIn or Twitter presence a human face and name — not a company name and logo — and a potential solution to offer.

     For example, Flo, the Progressive girl (remember, she has more than 4 million likes), is there to help you save money. Now mind you, they are also posting all kinds of fun content that is entertaining and engaging, and it's NOT always about car insurance. She talks about skiing in the winter, barbecues in the summer, and stuff she just finds interesting or funny. It's just the way it would be if she really were your friend.

2. Tell a story versus listing features and benefits.

3. Be brief and use plain language.

4. Make sure the fit is genuine. Don't put your message in a dialogue where it doesn't fit with what the group cares about. So if the conversation is about an upcoming social event or a party, don't say something that may be in context but kills the buzz, like: "I had a friend who went to a party one night and never made it home, leaving his wife and kids in financial ruin. Make sure your life insurance is up to date." (Classic Land Shark moment!)

A good way to test if your messaging is genuine is the level of emotional responses you are getting — good and bad. Remember the saying,

you always hurt the one you love. Real personalities create authentic responses. And authentic people are emotional. Resist the urge to create language that is so vanilla that people don't respond.

This is not your father's marketing campaign

How do you think innovatively about this? One of the most effective ways to ensure that you are doing social media well is to have someone from outside your industry take a look. If they tell you your approach is relevant and effective, then it probably is.

Who should this outside judge be? Someone who:

A.   is not in your business, BUT
B.   has a need for your product or service, AND
C.   is a heavy social media user, AND
D.   is in the target market, OR
E.   has dealt with a similar issue in another industry.

In the case of insurance, why not bring in people from your target segment to give you the honest truth about how engaging your social media presence is and how likely they are to go back to it? If you are in the life insurance industry, how about bringing in someone from Progressive or another P&C company, like Geico, to learn more about how to create a personality around your brand that is social media "ready"? How about someone from Redneck Bank, "where Bankin's Funner" **(yes, it is a real bank)**?

As a double check, you could bring in a comedian. No, really. Comedians are trained to point out what to them are obvious flaws in the way people and organizations view the world. What would comedians make fun of if they were looking at your communication?

But no matter what you do, the key is to start with the consumers' needs first! What are they really trying to solve that is real and relevant in their lives? If you don't know that intimately, the market will not believe what you have to say.

Things to do Monday morning:

☐ If you have a social media presence on Facebook or Twitter, ask yourself why you have it. Is it because it feels like something you have to do or is it because you have something social to say? If it is to check the box, lower your expectations of what should come from it.

☐ Look at your content. Is it about your products or is it about something that you believe in that will resonate with a wide audience? Is anything worthy of word of mouth? If not, rethink it.

☐ Look at your followers. Are they mostly your own employees or families of your employees? If so, consider what you can do to get your own customers more engaged.

☐ If you have hired someone just to post and tweet messages that push your product and brand, stop. Go back to the innovation drawing board and come up with things that will "pull" (see Part 2), and then rethink your social media strategy around that.

☐ Don't take yourself so seriously. What are you doing that is worthy of making fun of? Maybe it's time to do so. Who knows? Your consumers may love the self-awareness. Or if it turns out that it is not that funny – eliminate it.

CHAPTER 12

Creating relevance: What Nintendo figured out about people who don't play video games — and what we can learn from Nintendo

Sometimes there are huge opportunities that we cannot see, either because we don't understand the market well enough or because we have not defined our business well enough.

I am fascinated by what Nintendo did when they invented the Wii. They went after "nongamers" — people who don't play video games. Some thought they were crazy. After all, if they don't play video games, how are they an attractive market for a video game company to target?

Well, Nintendo did at least two things that made this innovation effort a success. First, while competitors like Sony Playstation and Microsoft Xbox seemed to be obsessing over technology and graphics to appeal to the black belt gamers, Nintendo made sure it thoroughly understood ALL the attitudinal and behavioral segments of EVERY PART of the market.

Second, they redefined what they do for a living. (See our discussion in Chapter 1.) Do they make video games? Well, yes, but no. They do make video games, but they defined themselves as being much more than that. Nintendo said they are actually in the business of facilitating family entertainment.

That makes a huge difference.

What brought this home to me was thinking about my best friend. She and her husband have two young boys who master video games with the skill of a highly trained astronaut. The video games made by Nintendo keep them entertained, sometimes even quiet, which is a blessing.

However, if you ask their parents if they play those games, they say no. Why? Because they can't relate to them. They are complicated and intimidating, and they make you feel stupid when you watch your 5-year-old racking up high scores and you can't break into triple digits.

But what's more important than spending time with your kids? Not much. Nintendo saw that. They created Wii—a product that had games that all ages could relate to. They made the controllers look like the ever-familiar TV remote control. And they even made them white— far less intimidating than something looking like it came from Darth Vader's spaceship.

Now, all these "nongamers" are playing video games, but more important, they are connecting with their families in a way that makes everyone feel good!

If you look hard, you'll find lots of examples of companies that have looked away from heavy users to create even bigger markets. Tennis shoes used to be just for athletes; motorcycles used to be just for bad boys; and surgery used to be just for sick people.

What the heck does a video game (or tennis shoe) have to do with insurance or other "sold, not bought" products? Well, this is difficult, but someone has to say it. So I will.

Inside or outside the funnel?

I'm sick of focusing on the typical triggers of why people buy life insurance. I think you should be too.

Let's examine what I mean by "trigger people" — people who have a reason to think about life insurance. They just got married. They just had a baby. They just bought a house. They just had someone close to them die or become disabled. It's logical and right to think about insurance in these situations. And they should and usually do, and sometimes they actually go out and buy some insurance.

But how many people fall outside of that category? I don't know the exact numbers, but I would venture to say it is very large — far larger than people who find themselves in the categories I just talked about. In the

vernacular of Nintendo's example, I would call those nontrigger people "nongamers." They consider the product irrelevant to them.

WWND?

If we were to ask the question "WWND? **(What would Nintendo do?)**" (see Part 5 for more about this approach), we would probably revert back to at least the two great things that led to their breakthrough.

We'd spend a lot of time with people who don't buy our products to discover why they don't. Like, for example, they don't see an immediate need. And then we would redefine our business as a result of what we heard, just like Nintendo did as it morphed from a gaming company to a family entertainment one, broadening the definition of what they do.

What business do you think we are in? What business could we be in? How might that change what we see as a possibility?

The industry, as long as I've been in it anyway, has been building things and assuming that the trigger people will come. Suppose we went about it another way. Suppose we went to people who don't have insurance and ask what sorts of related things we could help them with. What risk-related tensions are still unsolved? Do they have to be the same kinds of risks we are already covering? Or, what can we do to help them see their own insurance needs more clearly? Maybe that would get us closer to defining our business as lifestyle continuity.

Things to do Monday morning:

☐ Look at your company's library of research and see if you can easily identify and articulate the key segments on which you are focusing, and why. If you can't, consider adding some studies that can get you to that point.

☐ If you are examining new product, service or business model ideas, check your ego at the door. And make sure you are NOT just checking a research box by doing a few focus groups, looking for some support and considering that an accurate test of the market.

☐ Consider the nongamer. How might you be able to redefine your business in such a way that includes people you are not selling to now? Remember, your agents are trained to look for certain triggers. Find people "outside your jar" who will be able to recognize behavior that should be significant to you but you are naturally missing. Are you too expert to see the opportunity here? I don't know who discovered water, but I'm pretty certain it wasn't a fish.

Part 4
INNOVATION IN A "SOLD, NOT BOUGHT" CATEGORY.

IS IT POSSIBLE?

CHAPTER 13

Creating an efficient and effective innovation process

There is a proven method to safely and consistently delivering game-changing ideas. And it doesn't start where you think. Every year, hundreds of millions of dollars – and thousands of jobs – are lost in what I call "the innovation abyss" – the place where seemingly promising new ideas go to their justifiable deaths.

While some industries or companies have mastered nailing the right insight and consistently delivering evolutionary or revolutionary ideas against it – creating the 10 percent of new products that actually succeed – others spend their time coming up with new products and services that are, at best, irrelevant and expensive and, at worst, career ending.

I have seen a growing number of insurance companies attack their innovation problem by throwing some smart people into a room and telling them to figure it out. I have news for you. It doesn't work. Titles like Chief Innovation Officer, or creating a separate "Skunkworks," is not what is called for. What works is a combination of a good process and the culture that supports it.

In this chapter, I will detail how industry-changing ideas and products are delivered into the marketplace. Simply put: The companies and marketers we see thrashing about don't fully understand how cost-effective innovation occurs. And even those who have had some success are usually starting in the wrong place and would be more successful – and far more profitable – if they modified their approach.

Let's start with talking about innovation in general, before moving on to discussing it in the insurance and financial services industries.

Where does innovation usually begin? With the product – the cool idea, the colorful gizmo whose ad copy writes itself, the paradigm-

shifting process with the PowerPoint presentation that draws applause from senior management. This is a flawed approach.

For example, somebody in R&D develops a cell phone that will allow you to make calls from the top of Mount Kilimanjaro to anywhere in the world. A bunch of really smart people sit in a room and decide that what this new Internet thing needs is its own online money to serve as an alternative to credit cards. Someone in the company says, "I have the perfect solution to the problem that there are too many cars on the road, and people are too darn lazy to walk short distances or take a bike. Why don't we create a two-wheel motorized scooter?"

What consumers eventually got, of course, was the Iridium phone, Flooz currency and the Segway.

In each case, the product did exactly what it was designed to do; the problem was that too few people cared.

The bigger takeaway: The companies that created these three products started in the wrong place. Let's take a small step backward to see why.

Where it all begins

How does industry-changing innovation happen? Innovation, as I said back in Chapter I, occurs at the synchronized intersection of:

1. a meaningful insight or market need,
2. a new product, service or business model that meets that need, and
3. communication that connects the two and allows commercialization to happen.

Think of that definition of a three-legged stool. Most companies successfully build only one or two of the legs, causing their innovation efforts to fail. You need all three to be successful. And you will be a lot more successful, and waste far less money, if you take the steps in order.

That's why you want to start by devoting a disproportionate amount of your time to discovering the market need. When I say disproportionate, I mean it. It is the most important of the three circles because it is usu-

ally the one that is either neglected or done incorrectly. In the insurance industry, it is clearly the weakest link of the three.

The best way to develop your next product efficiently is by figuring out what the market needs — more specifically, what the market needs that customers would readily accept coming from you, your brand or a company you could acquire. You already know the methods for doing that: Everything from market segmentation exercises to online panels and focus groups will help you come up with a market need. You should also infuse outside experts into all of these well-tested methodologies. Ask them to be part of the interaction, the data review and the insight development. They will help you see things that your expertise keeps you from seeing. They will help you come up with even more needs than you would on your own.

Now, take the most compelling insights and quantitatively test them to see which ones your customers tell you are the most valuable to them. While your favorite insight may not make the cut, you want to fish where the most fish are, so it is important that you focus your team on developing products against the needs that rank highest. That is intuitively obvious, of course. But the next step is not.

Matching the product to the market

When it comes to creating a product to fill the marketplace need they've discovered, companies often stumble at the same place: They get greedy and aim to have their product or service appeal to too wide of an audience. TiVo serves as a case in point. I am convinced that one reason it took so long to catch on and make money — and why it's now seen by many as just another form of DVR — is that the company was never clear about which need it was meeting.

The challenge for TiVo, like that for many other innovative products and services, is that it is capable of meeting too many different kinds of needs. It can record whatever show you want it to, so it replaces your VCR (you remember the VCR, right?). It can anticipate and find shows that you may be interested in watching, so it replaces your best friend's

recommendations. It allows you to skip over commercials, so it gives you more time to do the things you love to do. These are just a few of the many, many benefits of owning a TiVo, and they all sound great – too great, as it turns out. For the longest time, the company tried to promote all of its features – presumably to appeal to as many people as possible – and wound up confusing the masses.

By the time TiVo discovered that perhaps its strongest selling feature was that it was easier to use than a VCR, it had squandered tremendous momentum. If marketers had focused on a single insight/need and let reviewers and consumers discover all of the other benefits on their own, TiVo – a great product – would likely have dominated the market. I believe by properly quantifying insights, the company would have been able to avoid this incredibly costly and common error.

So not only do you have to create a product or service that meets the marketplace need you have discovered, you must make sure that customers understand that is what you have done.

Get the message out

I mean this with all sincerity: Insurance is one of the most innovative industries. The fact that your first reaction was "Huh?" or "You must be kidding" underscores our ongoing inability to effectively tell the world how we have created products and services to meet everyone's needs. But there's no denying the industry's track record. You want to figure out a way to leave money to your heirs (when you don't have a lot), or replace the annual pension your company has eliminated, or induce a really smart businessperson to join your board (when *she* is petrified she will be sued if *you* make a dumb decision). The industry has a product for you (respectively: life insurance, immediate annuities, and directors and officers liability insurance). In fact, it could be argued that innovation itself is only possible because of insurance. Why? Because innovation requires failure, and failure requires risk. Many companies will not engage in the appropriate and necessary amount of risk unless they know there is a safety net like insurance.

We have amazing products that we just don't communicate well.

The fact that we are poor communicators about all this is, unfortunately, not unusual. Poorly executed messaging often overwhelms the best insights and products. How to get around this problem? Three ideas:

Press 1 for English. Ask some potential clients at random to explain what "Universal Life," "Variable Life" and "Whole Life" are and the differences between them. I will be shocked if 3 percent of the people get it (sort of) right. Like most industries, insurance often forgets that its professionals are the only ones who understand its language. You want to talk to your customers using the words and terms they do in describing your offering. (See Chapter 10.) Additionally, maybe it is time to start explaining the gist of how insurance works (i.e., pools and probability and all that fun stuff) versus just features and benefits of any given product. When consumers don't understand an offering, they might assume they are being ripped off.

Get the benefit right. This is similar to the TiVo problem. TiVo couldn't figure out what benefit to stress; the insurance industry can't decide how to describe them. They aren't selling "life insurance" — they are selling "making sure your spouse is taken care of and the kids can go to college" protection. When companies connect the correct insight/benefit to the product and communicate the benefit evocatively, something magical happens. It sells. Cash value is a nice side benefit, but it is not the main reason for buying life insurance. If you or any of your sales reps don't believe this, recall the fun we all had in the '90s when the fashionable new suit called the "class action" was introduced because people didn't know they bought life insurance. Ouch. The industry is still smarting from that one.

Engage the influencers. Now, more than ever, social media allows us to find those who really care the most and get them engaged in our new idea. We can ask for their insights about how to communicate it and give them credit. Make them evangelists and carriers of the message. Once your campaign starts, they will be invested in it and help propel it. In the case of insurance, what kinds of people are we talking about? Well, insurance agents, of course, but also CPAs, attorneys, bankers

and financial planners — all the people to whom we turn when we have financial questions.

Innovating successfully is hard enough without getting in our own way. Following these three steps in order will make innovating more efficient (read: less costly) and will put you substantially ahead despite economic conditions.

Things to do Monday morning:

☐ If you have an innovation officer or an innovation skunkworks team, let them off the hook of figuring it out for themselves. Offer them proven methodologies. (For more, refer to **Brand New: Solving the Innovation Paradox**, published by Wiley.)

☐ Stop using focus groups to prove your idea is right. You can get anyone who you pay $150 to and give them free M&M's® to say they like insurance. Focus on insights first.

☐ Fire the kitchen sink. That is, any product idea that doesn't have one headline benefit should be disallowed. Go through the communication and sales strategies for all your products and readjust the ones that do not have a clear, singular benefit.

☐ Lose the notion that products are markets. There is no such thing as a "universal life market" or a "term market." Segments of people are markets. Their attitudes and behaviors make them distinct. If you start thinking this way, true insight is developed a lot more effectively.

CHAPTER 14

Building your innovation portfolio

One key reason our industry has so much trouble changing is because the people who promote the status quo are rewarded more than the brave souls who truly innovate.

The solution? Readjust our priorities. We need to understand that, without a constant stream of new ideas, we are doomed to be viewed as offering a commodity product. As the industry is slowly beginning to realize, there is no movement, market or margin in commodity products.

When you build a team that knows how to correctly balance the four categories into which your innovations naturally fall, you'll receive the highest possible return on your innovation portfolio. You'll also create a culture that knows how to move a market.

In this chapter, I will show you exactly how to do both.

When it comes to how you divvy up your personal investments, you have always (correctly) been told that they should be spread among asset classes (stocks, bonds and cash) and then diversified further within the classes themselves. For example, you might hold stocks in both foreign companies and domestic ones, shares of small retailers and big high-tech companies, and every member of the S&P 500.

Stop for a second and answer this question: How much money do you have? Good. Now answer a second question: Do you know exactly where it is invested right now?

OK, now the tough one: Have you balanced your financial portfolio recently (moving money from stocks into bonds; cash into stocks; whatever)?

Whether the answer to that third question is yes or no, the fact that you can even answer the question means that you have an idea of how much money you have and how you have it invested. That's always a good thing.

So, here is a similar line of questioning: How many ideas do you have? Do you know where your ideas are right now (i.e., do you know what categories into which they fall? Line extensions; concepts that will up-end your industry; something that could be really cool, but you are just not certain anyone is going to buy it, etc.)? How much money and resources are you putting in against each?

Sadly, when I ask these questions to even leaders who pride themselves on running innovative companies, I almost always get an embarrassed stare. They can readily talk about two or three projects currently in the works, but when it comes to their entire pipeline — their whole portfolio of new ideas — they are at a loss when asked to classify what categories into which they fall.

Herein lies a significant opportunity. You want to be diversified, and diversified effectively. The idea is to capture all the potential gains out there — the more bets you place, the greater the chances you have of being right — while minimizing risk. It's just like in personal financial planning. For example, if your investments in the small-cap growth stocks sector tanks, your bond holdings and money market funds might mitigate the loss, providing you are fully diversified.

Well, you can use exactly the same cover-all-your-bases-efficiently-and-effectively approach when it comes to innovation. Think of your ideas, budget dollars and people's time as assets in determining whether or not to invest in research and development, product tweaks, line extensions or new offerings — diversify them, as well.

Why? Invariably, the new things you are working on present different levels of risk and reward trade-offs. Like stocks, bonds and cash, they are not necessarily correlated to one another; the success of one is not contingent on another. By investing in each part of your portfolio, you will be creating financial and behavioral (more on this in a minute) diversification that will pay dividends today and into the future.

The obvious conclusion: As with financial planning, the idea of hedging your bets — while making sure you are represented in every important sector — makes perfect sense.

Please note: *Before you read any further, here's a prediction: Most everything you are currently calling innovation is going to fall into the evolutionary quadrant. This is like saying you are a seasoned investor, but you are putting all your money into bonds. Yes, you are investing, but no, you are not going to get the returns you may be promising to your staff and investors.*

The four classes of innovation

If you want to go down the road of diversifying your innovation investments (and by this point, you have figured out I think you should), the obvious question to ask is how should you divvy up your portfolio? Before you can answer that, you need to determine the classes into which your innovation efforts fall. There are four. (After I describe each, I'll outline some benefits and challenges that each innovation quadrant brings.) But first, let's discuss the quadrants:

1. Evolutionary Innovation

(Technically easy with a clear customer benefit. "They are asking for it, we know how to do it, so let's give it to them.") Please note that word "they." Your agents are not your customers. Even here when you are playing it safe by simply adding small requested nuances to a product or service that are easy to do, you may miss the mark if you are responding to the wrong "customer."

This is the effort you extend to keep current cash cows fresh and to grow brands in the market. It's a hedge against becoming stale. It is generally the largest portion of any company's development budget, and it's sometimes overweighted in organizations that tend to "follow." (Companies like the clothing retailers you find in the mall don't tend to create new fashion trends. They wait until something gets hot and then they introduce a variation very quickly.) Examples of evolutionary innovation would include combining DVR functions into a cable box, launching a new flavor of an existing product, or anything that you can label "new and improved." In the insurance world, this could be a rider that may add an additional

benefit for a certain kind of accident or disability, as an example. This is a place where you listen to your customers — and give them what they want. Although the practice of creating evolutionary innovation can be relatively clear-cut, please be aware that it is a full-time job when done correctly. *So if you are wanting every member of your team to work on every quadrant, you are absolutely asking too much of them.*

Pros of the Evolutionary Quadrant

- Evolutionary creates a culture that actively listens to customers and consumers.
- Ideas can and should come from anyone with customer contact. That can be energizing for all levels of the organization.
- Since your ear is always to the ground, you quickly know when something in the market is changing.

Evolutionary Innovation Watchouts

- If this is all your team does to innovate, you will be doing all your negotiations with customers with a "procurement" mindset because you will only be competing on price.
- This can be mind-numbingly boring work, and you will likely lose the attention of your best thinkers.

2. Differentiation Innovation

(Technically difficult but a clear customer benefit. "They are asking for it, we have no idea how to deliver it, but we'd better figure it out.") This portion of your innovation budget is used to make a distinction between your products and those of your competitors. Multitouch interfaces were studied for years. Apple took on the technical challenge to put it into a mobile phone, eliminating the need for a traditional keyboard, and the iPhone went on to be one of the most successful products of all time. In the insurance industry, I often think of the direct term insurance providers (i.e., SelectQuote, Matrix Direct, AccuQuote) that offer products from many insurance companies and have created a model to allow term

insurance to be bought "mostly" online. While there are some things that still need to be done face to face (like medicals), the "feel" is as though it was bought online. That was a major differentiator.

Pros of the Differentiation Quadrant
- Differentiation creates a learning culture
- Differentiation means you can command a higher price.

Differentiation Innovation Watchouts
- Striving for perfection before you launch an idea burns out the best thinkers.
- This is the Achilles Heel of large organizations. Be careful that your people aren't using research as a risk shield here. ("I know we are nine months past our deadline, but there are still two more field studies we want to do to make sure we have dotted every 'i'.")
- When I see an overabundance of ideas in this quadrant and still see poor performance in the market, it usually indicates that the culture is afraid to fail. People are literally overtesting ideas — or worse — dumbing them down to the point where they scare nobody. This means that they are also no longer compelling enough to excite your customers.

3. Revolutionary Innovation

(Technically difficult and there's no way of knowing ahead of time if the customer will accept it. "We don't know if we're on the right track, but if we can figure this out, we think we could change everything!") This is the place where you search to find groundbreaking ideas for products, services and business models. PayPal, iRobot's Roomba (the robot vacuum cleaner) and Fuji's environmentally safe batteries would be examples. This is a bet that the market will move toward your idea and your company will have a sustainable first-mover advantage. If I were to think of a revolutionary insurance idea that has been created in a "sold, not bought" category, I would say the idea of accelerated death benefits in life insurance.

Pros of the Revolutionary Quadrant
- The biggest thinkers in the organization find this quadrant absolutely inspiring. Work in this quadrant typically unearths insights and ideas that feed the other quadrants.
- You are swinging for the fences, so if you get a hold of a good idea, you will change your industry and potentially garner HUGE returns.

Revolutionary Innovation Watchouts
- This is a sexy place to play, but if it is all your teams are working on, chances are that you will run out of money before you find the big idea.
- This is where a lot of dot-gones went.

4. Fast-Fail Innovation

(Technically easy but no way of knowing if the customer will accept it. "We have this amazingly cool gizmo, and I think/hope/bet somebody, somewhere will really love it.") This is an approach where you go to market and do your testing and learning there. It is the opportunistic segment of your development activities (i.e., it's well within your wheelhouse of capabilities and core competencies but far more experimental than usual). Here you expect to fail quickly before succeeding with an offering that is refined by your customers' feedback. It is fairly low risk; you don't spend much time or money before you send the product out into the marketplace; and it has an extremely high potential reward as customers express exactly how they want you to alter your original idea. Google runs multiple tests on ads it is considering using and then goes worldwide with the ones that work best. Often this quadrant involves partnerships where one side provides a missing ingredient, like a brand, a channel or a technology, to the firm that had the idea. For example, P&G teamed with its rival Clorox to create ForceFlex® Trash bags. P&G already had the plastic technology that made it possible to create stronger and more flexible garbage bags. Clorox had the brand name – Glad. The union helped Clorox create a billion dollar brand. While "sold, not bought" categories are not as excit-

ing as trash bags, there are examples where fast-fail innovation has been applied. Trash bags are a good example of an industry that attacked what consumers "hated" in order to innovate (e.g., I hate that my bag rips; I hate that it doesn't fit in the can; I hate that I can't find the opening of the bag; I hate that I can't tie it up easily). What do people hate about insurance?

Here's another example to spur your thinking: Affinity programs where a company enters new markets by partnering with credit card companies or large employers to offer insurance products on a large scale to their member/subscriber/employee audiences in a co-branded fashion. They are basically selling what they already have but trying it on a market with which they are not familiar.

Pros of the Fast-Fail Quadrant

- This is a great place to exercise R&D demons. Those guys in the lab coats have all kinds of cool innovations just looking for a market. Insurance marketers do this, too, but they don't wear lab coats; they wear those funky eyeglasses that distinguish them from other roles in the company. But, nonetheless, they strive to find new markets for the products that already exist.
- You create a culture that is always looking for win/win scenarios in the market. Your people begin to look for cocreation partners.
- You make it OK to take calculated risks, fail and learn. This is essentially an antidote for the biggest challenge with the differentiation quadrant: fear of failure.

People support what they create. If you can find partners who can provide new channels, complementary capabilities or some other things that you need to launch a new product or service and build something new TOGETHER, you will never have to sell this idea to them because it is their idea, too. Imagine going to Wal-Mart and building a new insurance offering **with them**. This cocreation formula is driving some of the biggest new offerings we see today.

Fast-Fail Innovation Watchouts
- As I have discussed throughout, it is always best to start with a need and follow with an idea. This quadrant typically starts with an idea and looks for a need. This is a less efficient way of innovating. That is why you want to make it fast fail (i.e., you don't want to spend a whole lot of money up front). You want to get out into the marketplace and see what happens.

> Who owns a Snuggie®? More than 30 million have now been sold. Unbelievable! Direct response marketing has mastered the ability to micro test ideas like the Snuggie—ideas that would have been summarily rejected if they could not be tested efficiently. Look at their model for a ready-made way of doing this in your company.

So how do you divide it up?

Now that you understand your innovation "asset classes," where should you focus your attention? How exactly do you divide up your portfolio?

> You want to overweight certain portions of your innovation portfolio. The evolutionary and fast-fail segments have the highest potential returns for your **internal** innovation group because they can get to "go" or "no-go" decisions much more quickly.

Well, with the caveat that no two companies are the same, I'd have to say that the fast-fail and evolutionary quadrants merit the most attention. (You need to have faith in your team's ability to use customer and sales force feedback to fill your pipeline with evolutionary and fast-fail ideas.) That's why in the hypothetical model, depicted by the graphic later in this chapter, it is devoting 75 percent of the resources to those two categories.

There is a second reason I like dividing up your innovation portfolio this way. These two quadrants provide a healthy balance:
- One has you listening deeply to your current customers, while the other opens you to the possibility that there may be partners who can provide you with new customers and new insights.

- One quadrant focuses on things you are sure about, while the other focuses on things you are not so sure about.

Both quadrants provide rich ground for training, coaching and fun boot camp-like experiences that will allow you to create a culture that knows how to repeatedly innovate.

And both quadrants offer your team the opportunity to quickly get to answers that green or red light initiatives. There is little time wasted. And the only thing more valuable than money, when it comes to innovation, is time (as in speed to market).

Am I diminishing the importance of the other two quadrants? No. But they are more risky. They are more time intensive and often have some side effects that are cancerous. For example, by far the biggest challenge with the differentiation quadrant is overthinking. I've seen too many companies test and test and test concepts. By the time they launch, the ideas are either too dumbed-down (they offend nobody) or too late (the competition is in the market with their iteration of the product). Frankly, many organizations have leaders who use this quadrant as an excuse NOT to launch ideas. They won't sell something until it is perfect and, well, nothing is perfect. Their thinking is "if we never go to market, there is no way we can fail." The sad fact is that in these kinds of companies, it is safer NOT to launch than it is to launch.

At the risk of offending some folks, I see a trend that when well-seasoned executives are put in charge of innovation, they typically wind up spending much of their time in this quadrant because their real expertise is proving that ideas won't work.

When you see people rolling their eyes when the word "innovation" is mentioned, it is usually because they have had experience with an organization that is stuck in the maddening cycle of test, test and test some more...with very few ideas ever actually launching.

The simple solution here is to reward people for launching failures as well as in-market success. Another solution is to leave this quadrant to outside consultants who are objective and compensated for taking the risks that your people cannot.

As for revolutionary products, we'd all like to create something like the iPod, but these ideas are, by definition, game changing, so they most often come from entrepreneurial companies and people currently outside your industry who aren't constrained by your paradigms, fears, politics, etc.

I love, love, LOVE the concept of war games here. On a number of occasions, Maddock Douglas has been hired to literally play the role of competitor and create ideas that will "put us out of business in one to three years." Imagine the drama when we present ideas — complete with quantitative data as your competitor — that make your executive team want to wet their pants. And imagine the relief when you tell the team that these ideas belong to you (i.e., them, since they hired us).

You don't want to abandon this quadrant altogether, however. Working on revolutionary products is inspiring, is energizing and invariably creates new products inadvertently. Think NASA. (The cliché is always to mention Tang and pens that write upside down when thinking about all the products that were created as a result of the space program. The list is truly remarkable.) NASA has received more than 6,300 patents. See http://www.sti.nasa.gov/tto/.) Tang is great, but I don't see a life insurance company getting into the soft drink business. Wait! An insurer could actually get into the healthy home business, insuring air quality, water quality... but I digress.

A SIMPLE RULE:

Evolutionary innovation should come from inside your halls and revolutionary from outside your walls.

Given everything I said, the odds are you will want to allocate your innovation assets this way:

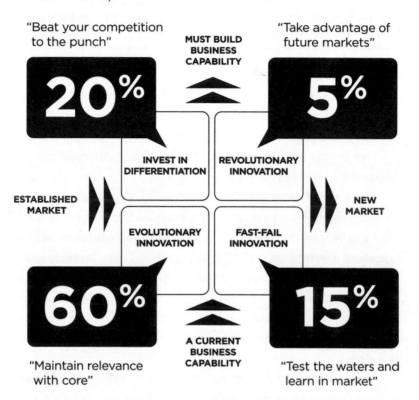

In more aggressive industries (i.e., sectors such as consumer electronics that live and die by new products), your innovation portfolio development model might see a higher balance of effort in the upper right side of the diagram (revolutionary) and less on the upper left (differentiation). In more conservative industries, it's vice versa. One size does not fit all, but the model above is a good starting point. The insurance industry doesn't necessarily have to match this allocation exactly, but suffice it to say that the allocation today is probably close to 90 percent (I was right, wasn't I?) in the evolutionary category. To stay relevant, more should be put into the other three.

We often hear that leaders want their organizations to behave more like entrepreneurs. We have done extensive research, and it should be no surprise that entrepreneurs spend much more of their resources on the top two quadrants. Why? Risk correlates with margin.

Putting the idea to work

I talked about how you are probably going to spend a disproportionate amount of your innovation budget on evolutionary and fast-fail ideas. Here, let's talk about how you can beef up that portion of your pipeline.

Evolutionary first. Here are two simple techniques to make sure you have plenty of evolutionary ideas:

Employ VOS brainstorms. We've all heard of the voice of the customer research, where you capture customers' wants, wishes, desires and expectations (plus the things they hate, so you know what to avoid). But how about the voice of sales? Typically, nobody has more immediate and relevant feedback than your frontline salespeople. They can create the outcome you want.

People support what they create, so make sure your sales team has a fun and consistent process for creating evolutionary product and service ideas.

One caveat: If members of your sales team are highly commissioned, they may hold on too tightly to products or services with higher rates, even when your customers are seeking alternatives. It is important to recognize that yesterday's commission models were created with a very different consumer dynamic. As I've talked about repeatedly, consumers used to get their information and messaging from advisors primarily and maybe an ad or two. Today, there is an abundance of information available from websites, financial personalities, DIY books and so forth. Many consumers are questioning why the rep's commission is so high if they, the customers, are doing most of the work of figuring out what they need. (See Chapter 6 on prosumer.) This could give rise to considering new commission structures for the sale of products and services. Again, stay focused on solving for the customer need.

Eavesdrop. It's rumored that, in the early years, Michael Dell would have his call centers keep small notes on all customer feedback. Dell would take the notes, spread them on a table and read them like tea leaves; then he would create services and products in response to what he saw. Auditing your call center, attending research sessions and participating in online discussion boards are all simple, proven ways to hear customer/channel/distributor needs. When was the last time you bought what you sell from someone who didn't know you were in the industry?

Here's a build on the idea: Don't listen alone. Bring along an expert "listener" or two from outside your industry. (See our discussion on "parallel engineering" in Chapter 3.) They will hear things differently from the way you do and point you toward simple opportunities you may otherwise miss.

On to the second quadrant: fast fail. If you manage it correctly, it is fairly low risk — you don't spend much before you send the product out into the marketplace — and it has an extremely high potential reward as customers express exactly how they want you to alter it. Here are two ideas on how to do it.

Rapid prototyping. One of the best ways to test an idea is to find a company that can launch the concept regionally and would love to do so because it complements its services, products or brand. You get in-market data and a partner that gives you momentum and future options. This technique allows you to quickly assess and profit from ideas you don't have time to manage. It even allows you to broaden your portfolio by investing in or selling great ideas that don't fit your model or brand. Consider testing in perhaps one or two states to get a read on demand — perhaps in a state with more lenient regulations so you are not as hung up in paperwork.

Here's an example of what I am talking about: *Redbox*, which has vending machines that rent movies, started as an idea within McDonald's. It tested well and wound up being a great business the hamburger chain's venture arm decided to cash in on by selling. (And you will notice how they [successfully as it turned out] partnered with other companies when it came time to test the idea. They put the movie vending machines in

supermarkets.) Redbox now has more "locations" than McDonald's and Starbucks combined. They are moving beyond selling movies because they recognize their enormous channel potential and the impending shift in their current market. Is there an insurance product that could be sold through Redbox? Your brow is now furrowed. But I promise you that you will eventually see completely unexpected things successfully sold through Redbox machines, and if you are a (former) movie executive, rumor has it, you could be shocked again.

Budgeting

To take the financial planning metaphor one step further, automatic "rebalancing" is important, too. With your personal portfolio, once one portion of your assets becomes out of balance — stocks go on a nice run, and instead of making up two-thirds of your portfolio, they suddenly account for 75 percent — you readjust your holdings. (In that case, you would sell some of your stocks, putting the proceeds into bonds and cash to get you back to the allocation you want.)

It's no different here. Once an idea develops in the revolutionary or fast-fail quadrant, you probably want to move it to the evolutionary box after it grows and matures. The budget should be adjusted accordingly.

Once you have this system in place, you and your team will be able to literally prioritize your next innovation initiatives based on what your portfolio needs. (e.g., "We're going to focus on project Firefly next because we need another differentiated project.")

And speaking of budgets, the nice thing about approaching innovation this way is that it makes the budgeting process substantially easier. There are fewer fights over funding someone's pet project, or chasing the current hot trend. Funding becomes strategic. You have your innovation asset allocation model, and you divide the money up accordingly. This reduces stress at budget time by getting everyone thinking the same way about how to set priorities. It allows your team to stay focused on generating the right ideas and then implementing them, versus the hamster-wheel scenario of repeatedly guessing at the "How much should we

spend?" question (and it eliminates all the time wasted as people lobby for their favorite project).

The idea of borrowing successful ideas from one place (a TV show that worked in Great Britain; a consumer electronics product that is all the rage in Japan) and using it somewhere else (reworking that TV program for the U.S. market; modifying the consumer product to satisfy customers worldwide) is a very common practice in innovation. That's all you are doing here in borrowing the asset rebalance concept from financial planning.

Teaching your team to steal ideas is fundamental to becoming ninja innovators. But stealing is not a politically correct concept so, instead, teach them to **"parallel engineer"** ideas.

I suggest you go through the rebalancing exercise once a year. This will allow you to manage your people, your money and your ideas more intentionally. Although this may seem like a difficult task — and it may be the first time you undertake it — it can be done by asking your innovation team to report on all of the ideas/concepts in play.

Here are the specifics.

1. Meet with all innovation leaders in the company. These could be people with innovation titles but more likely those with responsibility for creating the new products, services or business models for the company. They could be marketers, actuaries, product managers, or even operations and systems leaders.

2. Ask them to present or talk about each of the new product, service or model concepts/ideas on which they are currently working.

3. Then ask the question: How do we know our customers/consumers want this? Then you can dig into the specifics of how much qualitative/quantitative research supports their opinion. (Sometimes their opinion is well founded, sometimes just a hunch.)

4. Finally, ask them this question: Is this something our company can easily do? If not, what stands in our way?

The answers to questions three and four will allow you to first place each concept in the proper quadrant because you now have a pretty good idea about true customer demand and your ability to execute.

For example:

- We know they want it, and we know we can do it (evolutionary).
- We know they want it, but we don't know (yet) how to do it (differentiation).
- We know we can do it, but we don't know if anyone wants it (fast fail).
- We don't know how to do it, and we don't know if anyone wants it (revolutionary).

Once you have all your ideas organized into the four quadrants, you easily can see where your portfolio is out of balance, which will help you guide your team.

DON'T THROW OUT THE PENNIES LYING ON THE FLOOR

Here's something not to do: Many companies will disregard a product or service because it does not fit their financial model. That is not a good idea. For example, just because you sell products priced at $200 and up, don't kill an idea that will only sell for $20. You may be able to find a partner like PayPal who can sell millions of units and give you a percentage of every sale with huge margins because it is happening outside your walls. Apple gets a nice percentage of every app that you buy. If they were stuck thinking, "We make computers and sell them for thousands of dollars apiece, so why would we care about a 99 cent app?" they would be turning their backs on hundreds of millions of dollars a year.

I know of at least one life insurer that created an alliance with a credit card company and received a very small fee for each card that was applied for by its policyholders. While there were many attempts to kill that program because it didn't fit the model, the bottom line showed millions of dollars a year in income with a relatively small cost of sale.

Take it online. There has never been an easier time to get a product out into the marketplace quickly, get customer feedback and refine it based on what you heard. The makers of cell phones do this all the time.

(What version is the iPhone on now?) You may want to consider doing these "soft launches" in various parts of the country if you don't have the reputation of Apple, where any product introduced anywhere becomes worldwide news overnight.

Things to do Monday morning:

☐ **Are you in balance?** If you can't, off the top of your head, name where the ideas you are currently working on fit within your overall innovation strategy, something is terribly wrong.

☐ **Play matchmaker.** Certain people have certain skills. In the same way you divide up your innovation portfolio, think about having people concentrate in the innovation quadrant that plays to their strengths.

Sometimes, within Maddock Douglas, we use a military analogy to think about what kind of soldier should run each quadrant. For evolutionary, you want a Field Captain — someone who has been with the organization for a long time, knows how things work, knows how to get things done, knows how to pull the right strings. For differentiation, you need a General — someone who can and will take strategic risks without fear of being demoted or even court-martialed. For revolutionary, you want the CIA. They literally work on secret ideas in a white building somewhere off your campus, then show up once a year to scare the snot out of you. And finally for the fast-fail quadrant, you want an entrepreneurial diplomat — someone who makes quick, calculated risks and is always looking to seek partners who can help him out.

☐ **A good idea is a good idea**...even if it is not a good idea for you. Farm it out, sell or joint venture the concepts you come up with that aren't necessarily a fit for your organization.

CHAPTER 15

Insight development: Your but(t) isn't sexy enough

This title is not about calling you ugly and saying that your mother dresses you funny. It's about one of the key realities it takes for innovation: coming up with a killer insight.

One of the easiest ways to find an unmet need in the marketplace is to listen to when consumers say the word "but." A sexy "but" can make you a lot of money **(even if no one is ever going to confuse you with a rock star or model).**

Here's an example of what I am talking about.

"I like to drink coffee all day because it tastes really good, but I can't stand the jittery feeling it gives me." The "but" creates the platform for innovation. If you solve it, you have come up with an idea that people may pay for. The "coffee but" is probably why Sanka, the first decaffeinated coffee, was invented. Now, if you notice, every decaf coffee pot in a diner or coffee shop has an orange handle **(Sanka's signature color).**

So a proven formula for coming up with an insight is:

I [statement of fact] **because** [reason], **but** [tension].

As in what we just saw: "**I** like to drink coffee all day **because** it tastes really good, **but** I can't stand the jittery feeling it gives me."

Let's take six common occurrences in our industry and see if there is a way to solve for the tension.

Situation #1: *Financial products and services are confusing, uninteresting and a touchy subject.*

INSIGHT: **"I would like to have a better plan for my finances because it will help me in the future, but the thought of doing it puts me to sleep because all this stuff is so boring."**

We are in an age where there is no tolerance for confusion and complexity. Today's consumer needs and wants transparency. (See my discussion in Chapter 9.) And there is even less acceptance for anything perceived as boring.

Can't we figure out a way to make this stuff interesting as well as accurate? How about using animation on our websites — avatars and lots of illustrations in our material. You get the idea.

Consider a new label: *Financial products and services are helpful, interesting and engaging.* The potential payoff? **Understanding may be the next competitive advantage.**

Situation #2: *Financial products are paralyzing.*

INSIGHT: **"I would like to have a better understanding of my financial picture because it will help me in my future, but I feel totally stupid when I try to figure things out."**

I've mentioned before that people are baffled by the industry's language. For example, very few people under the age of 35 were able to define the term "annuity." Many respondents also preferred "made up" insurance product names over the real ones. For example, they would like to buy "income coverage" versus "disability income insurance." "Income coverage," or "paycheck replacement coverage if you can't work," sounds better to me, too, if my only other choice was "disability coverage."

We need to think differently and ask different people some different questions about how to communicate complex things in a simple way. How about starting with product names? Perhaps we should name them for what they do versus what they are. A paycheck for life makes someone feel happier than an annuity. How about using visuals versus columns of

numbers and having THAT be a requirement? A diagram may be far easier to understand than the required sales illustration. How about getting some outside perspective? A graphic designer may have a very different solution than an actuary. Pictures, videos and storytelling techniques are taking over the world. Our children are reading less but taking in much more. The days of documentation and perhaps even books are numbered. What is your plan to get noticed by a generation brought up on video games?

Consider a new label: *Financial products and services instill positive emotions that make people want to take action.* The potential payoff: **People will want what we sell.**

Situation #3: *Financial companies avoid telling the truth.*

INSIGHT: "I would like to have an advisor help me with my finances because it will help me in my future, but I am afraid of getting ripped off."

Remember my discussion of synthetic CDOs in Chapter 9? Unfortunately, it is not the only financial product that is almost impossible to explain. Try telling people how Equity Indexed Universal Life Insurance – or any number of other ridiculously complex things we offer – works. Yikes.

A great test for whether or not a product or service adds value is to ask your customers who already bought it to describe it. See what they say. Is it more about how the thing works or who benefits from it? Would you be OK if their description was not the way your website read?

Consider a new label: *Financial companies are out for my best interests, and I can see it in the products that they are offering.* The potential payoff: **If people understand what we are selling, they may buy more.**

Situation #4: *People don't think they can be educated about financial matters.*

INSIGHT: "I would like to understand financial products because it will help me figure out what's right for me, but I would rather just have someone tell me what to do."

Fiduciary responsibility—a relationship where one person has the obligation of acting in the best financial interests of another—is one of the most important forms of trust that can exist in business relationships.

Yet, we use all this complicated language and technical jargon, and we employ techniques that do anything but help people understand what they are buying and how it works. Some may even argue that the "fine print" is a way to keep people from knowing the truth. Wouldn't this seem to fly in the face of fiduciary responsibility? There would seem to be an obligation to make people understand before they choose.

What are the best ways to find these disconnects and build a bridge between the familiar and the unfamiliar?

Here's a thought: Look for the places where people go "huh?" Observe the emotions that go along with it. Do people feel stupid or ashamed? Do they get angry at the communicator? Are they just truly indifferent? Do they really want to know the answer? Research here is important. Pay attention to what makes the "light bulb" go on.

Be careful here because many experts hear "huh?" as an affirmation that they are necessary. Innovators hear "huh?" as a gap in product or service offering that is ripe for change. For example, I heard a friend of mine searching for the words to describe "hedge fund manager," but instead she said "hedge hog." Perhaps this is because hedge hog is familiar, and the term contained one of the words she was searching for. Instead of laughing at it and correcting her, perhaps we should recognize that most people don't think of a "financial strategy" when they hear the word "hedge." Rather, they think of shrubbery. Perhaps calling it a see-saw fund or a long-short fund (hedge funds were started so that managers could go both long and short in the market) may have been a better choice. Of course, this sounds unsophisticated, but who are we trying to help here?

This is the place where you want to create a new way to communicate the product in a way that people "get it." Make sure it is a bridge to the purpose of the product and not to something that helps internal experts understand the differences between it and other products. If it's an investment offering, it should be about the philosophy, management and time horizon, not about the past returns. Otherwise, confusion is bound to get even worse when the performance isn't there. To use a really simple example to hammer home the point: Why wouldn't a consumer choose a "High Yield Bond Fund" versus a "Small Cap Stock Fund"? The world likes "high" better than "small," but these words have nothing to do with the information one needs to make a good decision, and nothing to do with each other. What about calling them "Higher Risk and Returns Over the Long Term" Funds or "Stocks of Smaller Companies" Funds. No, not sexy, but very descriptive.

Don't be surprised if we eventually see funds that describe the management more than the fund itself *(e.g., the serial entrepreneur fund or the Maverick Cowboy fund)*. There are already funds that are designed to appeal to specific segments such as Conscious Capitalists. These are great examples of flipping from what you are selling to who you are selling to.

Doing all of this is no easy task; however, no great opportunity is ever easy. Having a good process for discovering the insight is key.

Consider a new label: *Financial products and services are intuitive.* The potential payoff: **Providing financial literacy could be a source of competitive advantage.**

Situation #5: *Financial and insurance companies push products.*

INSIGHT: "I would like to have the right life insurance products because it will help me protect my family, but I feel they try to sell me more insurance than I need."

You don't want to be seen as a land shark. (See my discussion in Chapter 11.) If you are communicating with your customers and potential

customers, you want to be seen as offering information and products that are seen as appropriate and important to them. If you don't have anything of value to offer, don't communicate until you do.

We make this mistake over and over again in the life insurance world. There is a mandate to sell more of a certain type of product, so the product attributes find their way into mainstream advertising and promotion. For example, the exotic product called second-to-die life insurance was created primarily for paying the estate taxes of really wealthy people after the second person dies. The one percenters need that — maybe.

If you start putting ad messages for a product like this out to everyone, the majority of the world will go "huh?"

A few good rules of thumb for whether or not your offer is relevant are as follows:

1. Are you talking about something that feels routine or far-fetched? The more that feels routine, the better (i.e., if you are talking about the risk of death to an audience in their 30s, you are off base). (See Chapter 3 on this.) It may be time to consider that we can't lead with life insurance for certain audiences.

2. Does at least half your audience have a real need for the product, or are we using the ad media to reach the needle in the haystack (i.e., an ad about estate taxes on the radio during the morning drive)?

3. Are you placing the ad in a place that seems convenient and logical to you but doesn't seem to belong there from the consumer's point of view (i.e., a life insurance ad in social media)?

Consider a new label: *Financial services and insurance companies are relevant to me.* The potential payoff: **People will seek you out.**

Situation #6: *Financial education doesn't stick.*

INSIGHT: "I would like to have a better understanding of financial products because it will help me make better decisions, but I can't seem to retain what I learn."

We need people outside of finance and insurance to help us do something about this situation, especially for Gen Y.

At Maddock Douglas, we recognize that everyone is in some kind of jar. (See my discussion in Chapter 1.) And when we say everyone, we are including ourselves. Our imperative, as we get our clients to the point where they have a pipeline of innovative ideas, is to ensure we are always pulling ourselves and our clients out of that jar. How do we do that? Well, one of the most important ways is by infusing outsiders into the process along the way. Outsiders are not just random people, but they are picked for their expertise, which will usually have some challenge or element that is similar to the industry in which we are working. They can be scholars, business leaders, scientists, authors, artists — you name it.

Here are a couple of examples:

- For a client trying to innovate around life insurance distribution channel models, we involved a travel expert who has faced similar challenges in disintermediation.
- With a client in health care who is looking at creating a safe, comfortable environment for the elderly in their home, we involved a zookeeper who has to do the same thing for exotic animals.

So if I were trying to reform financial services, in addition to the technical experts and lawmakers, I would bring in poets, authors, musicians, preachers, artists and other creative right brainers to help explain these complex subjects in a simple and memorable way. Nobel prize winners have not been able to explain what we are offering, so maybe Grammy winners and Pulitzer Prize winners can.

For years, I have fantasized about a music video channel that would convey messages about financial instruments. I even created a prototype for it in my spare time. If you are interested, email me and I will send you one of those videos just so you can get the idea and give me feedback. ☺

flirting@maddockdouglas.com It was borne from my love of Sesame Street, Schoolhouse Rock and MTV. In fact, if you mashed the three of them together, you would get my idea: it is George TV™ named for the president on the $1 bill. It's based on the notion that music creates stickiness, and that if financial instruments could talk (or sing), what would they have to say about themselves that is neutral, unbiased and informing? Using familiar tunes is an imperative here because it helps the brain process the words without having to worry about where the music is going next. Think about it...if it weren't for "Twinkle Twinkle Little Star," very few of us would be able to remember the alphabet since most of us learned to chant the letters of the alphabet to the tune.

Consider a new label: *"Financial and insurance information is memorable."* The potential payoff: **People would remember to call us.**

Things to do Monday morning:

☐ Look for three things that your company is doing that perpetuate one of those old, outdated ways of looking at things. Change them – by the end of the day.

☐ Ask your compliance and legal departments to join you in the journey **(I am serious about this)**. Yes, it is hard, but if you can't inspire people who are playing for your own team, you may not understand this well enough yourself. (See Chapter 16 for more on silos and turf wars.)

☐ Put a jar in your conference room that accomplishes two goals. One is to remind you of the various limiting situations we find ourselves in when it comes to marketing. The second is that you should have people put a dollar (maybe $5) into the jar every time they use the compliance card. **It's pissing me off. Can you tell?** ☺

One more thing about this: The more you hold on to the idea that your industry is too regulated to innovate within, the more you are playing into the hands of a naïve and completely competent entrepreneur. In fact, if an idea angers you and you find yourself saying, "You CAN'T do that!" it's a sure sign that you have fallen into the same trap that has put countless experts out of business.

- You can't sell legal services online. **(wrong)**
- People will only buy cars from dealers. **(wrong)**
- Sick people go to hospitals and only doctors can treat them. **(wrong)**
- People will always go to colleges and universities for their education. **(nope)**

Are you too much of an expert to innovate in your category?

CHAPTER 16

Make turf, not war

The fact that "turf wars" exist in your company may not shock you. But from our experience, they are causing you to burn more resources than you can even imagine.

Turf wars occur when leaders from various disciplines in the company—either consciously or not—start measuring their success against peers in the organization, and not against their competition outside of it.

Turf wars insulate companies from real insights, and it makes failure punishable by death (or at least being replaced). Innovation can't exist without failure. Not the "stoopid" kind of failure (the kind with two O's). I'm talking about the kind of failure that allows you to learn a lot from your mistakes so that you can fix them in a hurry and try again. These kinds of failures get you closer to success and make the organization really smart.

Coming from more than two decades of experience in large corporations, and now having the chance to view them from a distance, I can say that there is likely more cognitive capital spent learning about what makes one's peers and superiors tick than what makes your customers tick.

And that kills innovation.

SMALL FAILURES WELCOME

The point of the headline above is simple: Failure Isn't fatal. In fact, it's **required** for innovation success—and indeed for corporate survival. Here's why.

1. Fear of failure is perhaps the worst affliction a manager can have, as management consultant and author James A. Autry once pointed out, "because it leads to creative paralysis and inhibited growth."
2. Lack of growth equals corporate death. The only way to grow is to try new things.
3. Common sense tells you the odds are ridiculously small that you are going to get your new product or service absolutely right the first time.

That means you are going to fail, maybe a lot, before you get it right.

You need to accept that fact if you are going to do your best work. It is a concept you must get across to your team and entire company in order to free them from the innovation-limiting shackles of perfection.

You need to tell them that the real failure is fear of launching an idea until it is perfect because, by then, the need you have identified may have been filled by someone else, or morphed into something new.

Far better is it to get the idea out there quickly, listen to what the customer has to say and modify it as necessary.

Yep, you could view all those modifications as evidence of failure, but you would be wrong. They are actually evidence that you are creating a company of "learners," not "knowers." A learning culture is an innovative culture. A knowing culture—one where everyone knows everything—is one in need of a new leader.

In a more moderate example, the silo mentality may not result in a turf war but in indifference. Apathy. Lack of support for an idea. And without the right support, a good idea will die like a plant dies without water.

What are the telltale signs of a siloed/turf-warring culture? Here are seven:

1. **Your innovative idea is met more with the reasons why it won't work** as opposed to how it could be made better. In the insurance industry, this is rampant. Often the compliance or regulatory excuse is used, and just about everyone accepts that. And when it is challenged, it becomes a turf war between the business and the legal department, not a partnership designed to solve consumer needs.

2. People only go to meetings about an idea if their boss tells them to go. This is a classic sign of a turf-warring culture because it means that people are not open to spending their resources on an idea that didn't come from their own area, or that is not directly related to their part of the business.

3. There are many pre-meeting meetings going on before an idea is raised so that there is agreement before there is any kind of public forum. This is clearly to avoid embarrassment at the meeting – a sign that even small failure is not permitted.

4. People use words and phrases like "my camp/your camp," "That's great, but I have to stay focused on...." "That initiative got Tom fired, remember?"

5. Meetings with the boss about some mundane issue always trump brainstorming or idea-sharing meetings with peers and subordinates that might foster innovation.

6. Ideas are named after the person who raised them... (i.e., referred to as "John's baby" versus coming from a group of people working together). If it is John's baby, then John gets either all the grief or all the glory, depending on the success of the idea. That's a huge risk for John, and for the organization.

7. Ideas are generated around profit or sales results versus consumer insights. For example, "we need to generate a double-digit ROI" versus "we need to do something to reach an underserved market" (profitability should be used as a screener, not an idea platform).

Turf wars must end, the silos must be broken and people need to support a culture of innovation.

So what are some of the ways you can do that?

A. Make sure ideas are attributed to efforts of the whole group. This requires a process for idea generation that allows everyone to build on them. If you follow this course, in the end, it's hard to remember who raised them. That's good because everyone shares the risk of failure and the glory of success.

If you can build ideas across groups (e.g., sales works with manufacturing to produce a new service), all the better. Remember: People support what they create.

B. The definition of a good idea – this is also known as success criteria – should be crafted and agreed upon (i.e., Does it align with a business goal? Is it insight driven? Does it fit the culture?, etc.).

Make sure that success criteria is built by all the key stakeholders. You should be able to say things like "Bob, we never would have even considered this idea if we hadn't thought seriously about your success criteria." You've just made it **(Cranky)** Bob's idea, too.

C. Failure must be accepted as part of the road to success. It must be rewarded in the right way. At Maddock Douglas, we reward failure first, by relabeling it "failing forward," and second, by giving an annual award to the person who took a smart risk, failed and the company learned the most from it.

D. The teams need a common rally point that conveys a spirit of who the company is to its CUSTOMER versus just what metrics they will achieve. Does the company want to be the choice for the savvy investor? Or the company that serves military people? Or is it the company that earned a 12 percent return?

E. Reward systems must account for team efforts.

F. Organizational structures should be more fluid and less hierarchical to encourage the "cross-pollination" of ideas that can benefit customers.

G. Consumer insight ("Sexy Butt" statements; see the last chapter) must be abundant and shared all over the organization. In addition to being critical, well-developed insights are very unifying.

We once had a client who had a reputation for pushing his spouse's ideas. You may have a boss who pushes his ideas. The beauty of good measurement tools is they quantify insight statements and concepts so that it is the consumer who is pushing his/her ideas.

The consumer must always be the strongest voice in the room. A great example of this is Victoria's Secret. She was a fictional character who represented the target segment. She had an address. She had fears and hopes. She was so well understood that all ideas were questioned through her perspective.

Innovative behavior starts at the top. Or to put it in the negative, the fish stinks from the head down. If you are struggling trying to figure out why innovative ideas are not coming from your company, ask yourself if silos/turf wars may be causing it. If so, it may be time for an innovation peace treaty—one that will call for recalibrating reward systems, developing the right behaviors, implementing innovation processes and ensuring that ideas are parented from start to finish. The most innovative brains in your company will see it as a breath of fresh air, and so will your bottom line.

Think of the poor customers here. Why should they have to be the victims of these turf wars by receiving multiple bills and statements? Even your distribution feels the pain. This tension is a very big one, and when someone solves it thoroughly (versus making everything just a little less obnoxious), the rest of the industry is going to have to get on board because the bar will have been reset.

Things to do Monday morning:

☐ Obliterate the words/phrases "my camp/your camp," "my side of the house/your side of the house," etc., that scream "I'm in competition with you!"

☐ Consider organizing around consumer segments versus products or distribution channels. At least that way everyone in a particular part of the organization is focused on the end user. (I know you've tried and failed at this, perhaps, but try again. The reason you failed is because of turf wars.)

☐ Leave your rank at the door when you brainstorm. Rank is useful in many business situations, but when it comes to innovating new ideas, different people have different skills and their rank means nothing.

☐ Take note if your team is spending more time running up and down the stairs to manage the expectations and perfecting presentations for a boss versus spending time developing insights and solving for market needs — even if that boss is you.

☐ Take note of the dynamics in cross-functional meetings. Let your stomach feel a little sick over how many people are introducing themselves to each other for the first time.

☐ If you are spending your own energy wondering what you need to do to look smarter to the people inside the organization, get smarter about the consumers outside your organization. It works wonders.

☐ Consider reframing failure. You are creating an entrepreneurial culture that knows how to learn quickly through smart experimentation.

CHAPTER 17

Love the one you're with: Innovation for the in-force

*In this chapter, I want to underscore that innovation is not just for the purpose of inventing **new** products, services and business models that attract new customers.*

While that is very important (and difficult), there is plenty of innovation opportunity when you focus on keeping in-force (i.e., your current) clients happy (and perhaps even delighted). This goes for the people who sold your product, as well.

The cross-sell/up-sell: Unprofitable or just unsexy?

Everyone knows it is easier and more profitable to get a larger share of a current customer's wallet than to acquire new customers. When you go to upgrade your phone, they automatically offer to upgrade your service plan (for more money of course). Your airline knows it when they ask you if you need a car or hotel when you book a flight. But insurance companies are not sure about this fact. Up-selling and cross-selling have befuddled the industry for years. Many try it but do not give it a high priority in the innovation pipeline. Or they give up completely when it doesn't produce results immediately. (The problem is definitely an outgrowth of the silo/turf wars discussed in the last chapter, in case that isn't obvious.)

> Having a single profit and loss statement for the entire organization will go a long way toward eliminating turf wars and spurring cross-selling and cross-functional innovation.

A recent study from the Chief Marketing Officer Council, a trade association, shows that 21 percent of insurance customers purchased or increased the value of their existing policies after receiving communica-

tions from their companies. Yet only 7 percent of these insurance market-ers said that up-sell and cross-sell tactics are critical for revenue.

Why the disconnect? In my experience, the marketers probably have questions about whether the increased sales are being double counted (i.e., there were two groups — sales and marketing perhaps — who are tak-ing credit for the same sale).

That's possible, of course. But is that the whole reason there is a lack of up- and cross-selling?

The thrill of the kill

Could it be that the distribution-centricity of the industry puts most of the emphasis on finding new people to sell to? Could it be that the pricing structures don't always lend themselves well to midstream adjust-ments, meaning that if current customers want a better rate — or to alter their coverage — they have to get an entirely new policy or leave for some-one else? For example, if customers bought a policy five years ago and now they want more coverage, sometimes they will be sold a brand new policy that replaces the old one completely because the new product has a better pricing structure (and maybe a new commission). That's all well and good, but they may lose some value in the process, like through surrender charges, or a lot of time (because they have to go through the entire underwriting process again).

Why not just give them the benefit of the new pricing from this point forward on their old policy?

Or perhaps the industry has just not been able to get out of its own habits long enough to see that today's consumers have changed, and that they want education and information and other value-added services from their insurance carrier, over and above the coverage that they are paying for. Can we develop something else that would be of value to help them become smarter about finances? Maybe a tool to enable under-standing? Maybe they would even pay for it? Perhaps the sellers of these products could benefit, too.

The legacy system problem

There is no doubt that one of the biggest challenges in the life insurance space is the legacy system – the one that was built to support the fact that some of our customers are with us for 50 years or more but not built to be able to work with the next generation(s) of technology. This is a tough one to solve because no matter what I say, it will sound easier said than done.

I concede the point. However, if you imagine your company as one that is incorporating today versus 150 years ago, how would you do it? What systems would you build to support the products and services you would want to provide today that allow your customers to feel like every product they buy from you is from the same company? How would you organize? How much would it cost?

It is helpful to look at what today's consumers expect. They expect you to know who they are, to know what they have bought and to automatically provide answers to all their questions (before they ask them based on their past history. Wasn't it just a few short years ago that everyone was so concerned about privacy issues? Privacy was used as an excuse to kill everything from personalized messaging to telematics. Now consumers get annoyed if basic information isn't understood by their technology and service providers – another great example of the rapidly changing needs of consumers.)

However, we are caught in a world where we will initially try to adjust current systems because it is too daunting to move all of that data over to a new one.

I can't argue with that. But what is the downside of not investing in the new technology? That's simple. Those who are new to the game could potentially invent a system that is much better at putting the customer in the center. They could quickly gain ground and put you out of business.

That may sound far-fetched because of the *seemingly* high barriers to entry in this business. But consider this...other industries have been reinvented by newbies. Netflix, LegalZoom, PetMeds, iTunes, Zipcar...they all have the same thing in common. At Maddock Douglas, we call this the

"Napster" moment. It is the moment where someone who has no business being in your business reinvents your business (and puts you out of business). Granted, Napster didn't succeed in getting rich, but they succeeded in changing the game for Apple to come and reinvent music. In the world of systems issues, this was a super duper extra large undertaking. But they didn't look at it that way; they looked at it as meeting a need the consumers had, which was to buy songs individually, instead of being forced to purchase albums that had cuts they didn't want. They could make individual playlists and mix CDs, which ties into the prosumer trend I talked about in Part 2. More music is being sold today than it ever was, but it is being bought differently. (See Part 5 for more on this.)

So if legacy systems are the issue for you, and you throw up your hands and say it is impossible, think about what someone who isn't in your business would do. Then do that before he does.

Things to do Monday morning:

☐ Make sure you really understand your CURRENT clients/ customers. Insights, again, are key. Perhaps you would find that there is an unsolved tension somewhere in the servicing area, or in their relationship with their advisors. Current clients have sexy butts, too! (See Chapter 15.)

☐ Bring in outsiders (Amazon; a cell phone company) who have nailed cross- and/or up-selling. Ask them what they have learned.

☐ Consider developing an idea pipeline that is designed to delight and retain your current clients above all else. Perhaps it includes an automatic change to a new product pricing structure that might benefit them? *(Actuaries are cringing right now.)* Maybe it involves inviting them to some kind of exclusive educational event about finance. Who knows?

While these three to-dos are far from covering everything you might do, I can guarantee that doing all of them well will put your company in a place to capture innovation opportunities that will give you a competitive advantage.

CHAPTER 18

Conclusion: OK, let's just DO it! (Innovate, that is.)

This chapter will help you frame how to look at innovation inside your company, presuming you want to get better at it. Here are things you can do to behave more innovatively every day.

While innovation and insurance are words not often seen in the same sentence, the tide is changing. The ever-present tension between short-range results and long-range planning has had an interesting impact on the demand for innovation. Today, just about every company in our industry is trying to ensure there is a solid pipeline of new ideas that can keep it moving ahead.

Perhaps the easiest way to think about this is to divide innovation into the four categories in which they naturally fall (as I discussed in Chapter 13). However, in this diagram, the motivations that go along with being "overweight" in certain categories are also included.

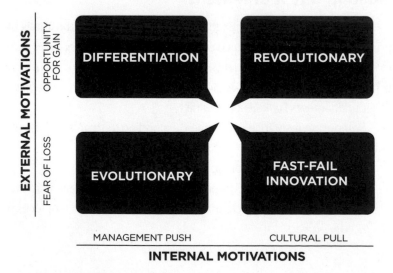

As you can see, the two quadrants on the bottom deal with fear. Fear is not a bad thing if it motivates short-term action. But protracted fear does not lead to sustained creativity and innovation. And creativity is very important. An *IBM study of 1,541 Insurance CEOs*, general managers and senior public officials from 28 countries shows they believe that creativity is more important than rigor, management, discipline, integrity and vision in a company's ability to remain ahead.

In a statement, IBM executive Mark Lewis said rising complexity, such as that induced by increased government intervention, requires insurance companies to be led with bold creativity and connect with customers in imaginative ways. You can't do that if you are afraid. When you allow a culture of fear, you are essentially asking your people to pay more attention to risk than to possibilities.

The attitude of innovative organizations is that failure is the key to deep learning. Learning becomes knowledge, and knowledge is an asset that is quickly becoming more valuable than sheer capital. So instead of "We failed…let's not do that again," it's "We failed, so we learned something that brings us a step closer to success…."

Getting ready for innovation: Build it, buy it or lease it?

While everything I just talked about makes sense, the most difficult part is getting started. Insurance companies are generally very well capitalized and willing to invest in the resources required for innovation, but it is not always clear where to spend in order to execute effectively against the four quadrants I talked about earlier.

So how are insurance companies responding to this? Well, basically in four ways:

1. Building an innovation discipline internally
2. Buying/acquiring a company known for its innovation discipline
3. Renting/borrowing expertise from a consulting firm for pieces of the process

4. Leasing/outsourcing the entire process and obtaining cultural training (for a period of time) from a company that provides "Agency of Innovation™" services

What are the benefits and pitfalls of each?

	Main Advantage(s)	Main Risk(s)
Building "Grass roots"	Resources are most controllable.	If the culture is not ready, these groups often get no traction, end up flying "under the radar," are seen as a threat or nuisance by the business units and become demotivated, having to "sell" their way in.
Buying "Going out and getting it"	The company retains ownership and control. It acquires expertise in a given field.	Often, the acquiring culture dominates, and the new company ends up losing its edge.
Renting "Gap filling"	Acquire pieces of the process via consultants to fill in perceived gaps. This is helpful for smaller budgets and shorter commitments.	Risk of losing continuity when the process is handed off from insiders to outsiders. Organizational learning can be hard to come by, meaning you will have to rent help over and over again.
Leasing "Learning with training wheels"	Learn the end-to-end process and experience without the risk of hiring employees. Get expertise from "outside the jar" (other industries).	Some of the resources are not in the company's control. Greater commitment of budget and time is required.

You need to pick the approach that is best for you.

Things to do Monday morning:

☐ Consider your organization's motivations. Are they more fear or opportunity based? Either is OK, but if it is more fear based, think about what you can do to help make it safer to be creative.

☐ Consider your process. Do you have one? If not, develop something that works for you and covers all the necessary bases.

☐ Consider your ideas and resources as innovation assets that need to be managed like investments.

☐ Consider your commitment to innovation. Is it to create a pipeline of new ideas or is it to transform your organization's culture to "speak" innovation? Knowing that will help you choose the best way to bring it to reality.

The process is designed to imagine the possibilities — possibilities that your competition may already be able to see. That's how we can create our own Napster moment (see the next chapter), and reinvent our business before someone else does.

Ready? Let's begin.

What would Mark Zuckerberg do? Leveraging the power of community visibility

There are certain signs our industry is ripe for revolution. Here I will discuss what revolutionary — as opposed to evolutionary — change is and point out that other industries — such as music, travel and mortgage — were disrupted in a blink of an eye. And for everyone who contends it couldn't happen in an industry like ours because it is so heavily regulated and because it is so complicated, I urge you to consider that those same elements existed in businesses that were reinvented.

Napster moments. In innovation terms, it is, as I said, when someone from THE OUTSIDE comes in and reinvents *your* game. Napster cleared the decks for Apple to own the music industry. Travelocity, Orbitz and Expedia reinvented travel. LegalZoom revolutionized legal services, and Netflix knocked out Blockbuster. I can name more… PetMeds, CarMax, Shutterfly….

I predict that the person who led one of the largest IPOs in history, *Time* magazine's 2010 Person of the Year, is going to reinvent the insurance industry. I am not sure if he knows this yet, but that's just because he is only now responsible for his own insurance coverage. (He qualified to be covered by his parents up until 2011.)

Mark Zuckerberg, who won't turn 30 until 2014, a) is the CEO of Facebook; b) is the 35th richest person in the U.S.; and c) has more than one billion users of his product. This means one out of every seven people *in the world* is on Facebook.

So why do I think he (or someone like him) will revolutionize insurance? That's simple. The insurance industry is facing challenges that make it ripe for a "Napster" moment. In our industry, the challenges are well known: fewer sales reps, increasing public scrutiny and regulations that nobody can seem to keep up with.

Inside our industry, many are looking to tangential industries, such as banking, investments and even retail, to find ideas that could help. That's fine. But when it comes to true reform, I am betting on a dark horse, like Zuckerberg.

His insight may sound like this:

"Insurance is important because it helps people continue with their lives as they want to when something bad happens, but insurance companies can't be trusted as much as one's own community can."

So why will Facebook, specifically, and social media, in general, totally upend our industry?

They have **three key elements that are required for insurance to work:**

1. A large, diverse pool of people. That's needed to spread the risk.
2. The ability to track and store large amounts of data and make predictions from it.
3. Social awareness of the burden of uninsured risks. People have to see that it is in the best interests of a community to have people be insured so they are not a burden on others. And, as we will see, young people today understand this.

And it has four things that **today's insurance industry does not have** but probably wishes that it did:

1. Significant levels of involvement and engagement by users
2. Viral marketing power
3. Instant feedback about what people like and dislike — and what is attracting the most attention at any given moment
4. A hedge against anti-selection (*Yes, all you actuaries, lean into this one.*)

Hang on to your hats

Here is a relevant piece of history that leads me to think the social media model could save our industry. Back before insurance was created, communities dealt with the threats of destitution with a method that was affectionately known as "pass the hat." When the breadwinner of a family died or became severely sick or injured, communities would respond by taking up collections to help the family get by, and thereby avoiding them becoming a burden on society.

In the 1700s, Lloyds of London had the idea to basically do this "in advance" of events instead of "in arrears," and the concept of insurance as we know it was born. It was such a benefit to society that the govern-ment later began to give incentives – including tax-free death benefits and buildup of cash value – for families to participate. Premiums were collected weekly by agents who went to the policyholder's home to col-lect the few cents that were owed.

What isn't spoken about much is that this system created significant social interaction and higher involvement in the product than is present today with more modern billing methods. The social aspect is what has gotten lost, and social networking has the ability to bring that back.

While most may say "who cares" about the social aspect, those people are missing an important point. Low involvement helps drive the negative perception about a product that people really need but many do not own.

Think about products and services you purchase that have low involvement – like getting an oil change or going to the dentist. Even when those experiences go well, there is not much positive emotion asso-ciated with them.

Many types of insurance, like life insurance, disability income insur-ance and long-term care insurance are very low-involvement products. Others like P&C and health may have slightly higher levels of involve-ment than the others, but still very low compared to other consumer products. There's no reason to engage unless forced to by the need for using the product or the need to transact a premium or other administra-tive change. That model stands in stark contrast to a product like a computer, as I said in Chapter 1. The consumer is highly involved, using it several times a day and doing so willingly, and being highly dependent on it.

But not only is the social media model one of high involvement, it is one that reaches a key market that we in the insurance industry have yet to figure out.

Boomeritis

As we saw, the life insurance industry's mission was one of creating an important social benefit. But while it is still important, our focus has veered substantially. We are now focusing on people who have money already, instead of those who do not who presumably would be the most in need of what we have to offer. In other words, the industry is concentrating on the boomers because boomers have the capital to put into insurance and presumably have the most at risk.

What about the under-30 crowd? Or the older Gen Yers who are now in their early 30s? Yes, it's true that they are not thinking about these risks as much as other things, and they don't have a lot of money. If you are to get into the heads of younger people, the insurance industry would define itself as being in the "lifestyle continuity" business, as I said in Chapter 1. That is, making sure that any risk of messing up their future plans is covered. It's not just about death; it's about life. If we limit ourselves to just discussing the one risk, and it doesn't feel top of mind, we are relegated to "noise." Recognizing what is a risk to a young person is critical for anyone to do something innovative in this area.

So what happens when a 20-something falls victim to one of these risks—like losing a job, or getting very sick, or wrecking their car, or losing their home—and they don't have insurance (and they probably don't)? They could go home to mom and dad, which is one option. But what if they don't have parents, or their parents don't have the means to help them? They turn to each other for help. And they are a generation of kids very willing to help those in need. They are interested in social good and sustainability. So they "pass the mobile device." They put their troubles out on Facebook and they ask for help. And often they get it, or their friends get it for them by setting up a special page for someone in need, and then going out to their networks for help, pledges, etc.

Suppose this ability was more formally structured and the method for collecting and distributing funds was simple.

Laughing all the way to the TelCo

More than $24 million was raised for Haitian relief after the earthquakes in January of 2010, and it was all done with text messaging in a matter of about a week's time. A bank never touched the money. The telecom companies were the ones that got to handle it for a moment — and received a small processing fee for doing so.

Now, if you combine that ability to collect and distribute funds quickly with the power of a social network, the "Napster" moment in insurance is born.

Hmmm, let's imagine for a minute how that future could look:

TODAY: We "pass the phone" to help underinsured people we don't know.

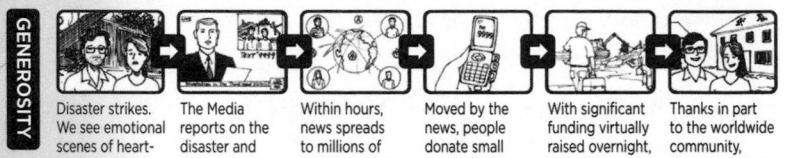

GENEROSITY

Disaster strikes. We see emotional scenes of heartbreak and loss.	The Media reports on the disaster and that you can text a donation.	Within hours, news spreads to millions of people via the World Wide Web.	Moved by the news, people donate small sums of money by sending a text on their cell phone.	With significant funding virtually raised overnight, financial and physical relief commences faster.	Thanks in part to the worldwide community, disaster victims return to normalcy.

TOMORROW: In advance of disaster, "insurance pools" are created to provide some level of coverage. The deficit—if any—is filled by mobilizing our social networks to help ourselves, our friends and neighbors.

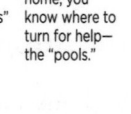

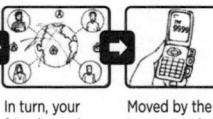

SOCIAL PROACTIVITY

Through social networks like Facebook, LinkedIn, churches, associations and communities, we create an "insurance pool."	Payments are very small and convenient— as simple as texting a number on your cell phone.	The more communities and networks with "insurance pools" you connect with, the more protected and confident you will feel...	...so when disaster hits home, you know where to turn for help— the "pools."	Your "insurance pool" agents— the catalysts— provide some immediate $$$ from their pool.	For any deficit, the agent sends e-alerts to friends in your network for support.

In turn, your friends reach out to their networks, too. Within hours, news spreads to thousands of people via the World Wide Web.	Moved by the news, people donate small sums of money by sending a text to a designated number on their cell phone.	With a percent of $$$ from your insurance "pools" and supplemental donations raised, financial and physical relief commences faster.	Thanks to both your insurance "catalyst" and your social networks, you return to normalcy sooner and more efficiently.

From anti-selection to self-selection

For all the actuaries who skipped over everything else just to get to this, here is your payoff. As social communities like Facebook begin to behave in a structured and organized manner, and they gain "claims experience," they will start to self-select people in and out of the pool based on their "social capital" (see Chapter 7), their responsible (or irresponsible) behavior and/or their contribution to the pool. So if Johnny has a bad driving record, his social community is going to require him to shape up, pay more or take less of a benefit.

Rachel Botsman, who writes on this topic, calls this kind of interaction/transaction "collaborative consumption" – renting, lending or even sharing goods instead of owning. And whether you are willing to do this with someone depends on their "social currency," your reputation.

This concept of collaborative consumption is fascinating and relevant to the concept of insurance and anti-selection.

Regulation, schmegulation

Insurance company leaders reading this would probably throw in the state regulation card as a reason why this idea would not work. However, in the Wiki/Wisdom of Crowds/Freakonomics/World is Flat/Tipping Point times we live in, I could see this emerging quickly and becoming the new model before states could define it as insurance.

Only someone who is from outside the industry will have the courage and ability to do this. Really. I can't think of a single industry expert (or single company for that matter) who would approach revitalizing our industry this way. Mark Zuckerberg would be perfect.

I am hoping that someone in the industry proves me wrong.

What would Massage Envy or a NYC cab do? Leveraging the power of social norms

This was an idea inspired by a visit with my friend Christi, who is also a veteran of the insurance industry. Luckily, we were able to expand our minds with a good bottle of French wine.

Here's a common tension we need to solve for:

"I would consider a career In insurance because it would give me the chance to be autonomous, but I wish I didn't have to starve on commission before I built my business."

What if the consumer was the one to determine how much an insurance producer ultimately got paid? **(Said under your breath, "yeah right,... but hmmm.")**

In today's model, producers are expected to work on commission from the get-go. In this new model, perhaps they could receive a small salary and have an initial upside in tips.

Would it work?

One school of thought would be that the producer would starve to death even faster because some consumers believe that existing commission schedules are already too high, and they are paying too much for insurance as a result.

But another might lean into the idea that today's consumers like to make their own choices, such as how much someone should be paid for taking care of them. And, oftentimes, they are making decisions based on social reasons, not just whether or not they like someone, or thought the person did an excellent job, but also based on social norms, like the rules of thumb for tipping.

How many times have you gone into a restaurant and tipped someone who you thought just gave you average service? Maybe even below average? Why do you do that? Because it is the "norm."

If you don't believe me, look at a few examples that have only gotten stronger with technology.

Today's NYC cab ride is probably as scary as it has ever been. Honestly, I feel I am sometimes putting my life into the hands of someone who is talking constantly but not to me. **(But let's leave that for a different day.)**

Yet, I would bet that tips are better than they ever have been. Why? Because of the options you are presented with at the end of your ride, if you pay by credit card.

The screen looks like this:

Suggesting tips of 15, 20 and 25 percent? That's how it started. Now it is 20, 25 and 30 percent.

The drivers got a raise just by adjusting a line or two of code to the automated payment system.

Sure, you could pay the bill by credit card or cash and tip whatever you like or nothing at all. But punching a button on a computer screen is easier than doing mental math, and people do not like to deviate from the social norm unless the circumstances are extenuating.

For example, I was in a very unusual situation with a limo service recently. The car was pulled over by the police, and the chauffeur was given a ticket for reckless driving. I was in the back seat, not only inconvenienced but somewhat concerned for my well-being. Despite the driver's tears and plea for forgiveness, I did not tip. But it took an authority figure (the cop) to validate the fact that my service was really bad. Had it not been for that, I probably would have left something. (And BTW, I hate to see grown men cry.)

Taking this example further, have you ever been to a Massage Envy? It's a great business model that gives members steep discounts for having at least one massage per month on a subscription basis. Massage Envy is a chain of mini-spas that do massages and facials. You pay about $59 per month, and you can get one massage a month or a facial with a small upcharge. If you want more than one a month, you pay another $59 for each additional one you want. If you are not a member, you pay $99 for each massage you get.

Employees put up a sign that suggests that members base their tips — tips you will notice that are assumed — based on the nonmember rate. They even go further and say that the "normal" tip for a nonmember is $20. If a member tips that much, the tip works out to be better than 33 percent.

Here's my point: People, as a rule, will do the socially correct thing. So, do you really think they would stiff the insurance agent if they knew he was working for tips?

I can use Mark Zuckerberg to make this point in the opposite way. The major news organizations had a field day reporting that he didn't tip for some meals while on his honeymoon in Rome, painting the billionaire as greedy. What they didn't report is that tipping is not the social norm in Italy. What appeared strange to Americans didn't really raise an eyebrow in Italy.

And if the insurance industry worked on tips, would we be able to price products differently? Would we be able to change pay structures of agents to give them small salaries and smooth out the lumpiness of their income, knowing that part of the cost is being paid for directly and willingly out of the client's pocket? Would we be able to attract a wider group of individuals to the job if that were the case?

After we had this thought in our heads, Christi and I went to dinner in the theatre district. Those waiters (also known as Broadway actors, in many cases) are very attractive, personable and convincing — people who need some kind of predictable income as they feed their dreams. Tips, you may say, are unpredictable, but not if you have a steady flow of people you are serving. In fact, quite the opposite. Could there be a whole new crop of people who are wired to do this already?

Hmmm. What could that model look like in real life? Well, it might take many forms, but suppose we stick with the Massage Envy parallel and see it all the way through. Perhaps an insurance company could create an online or bricks and mortar model that enabled people to gain some advice, education, coaching and reassurance from professionals who know the ins and outs of insurance. Suppose there were a subscription model where customers could be entitled to a certain number of advisory sessions per year, and they can do them via Skype or in person at a "store." It could be positioned as a "spa" for your financial well-being — a comfortable, inviting place where you could go to get all your personal finance questions answered and concerns resolved. Perhaps you walk in, there is soothing music playing, and your "therapist" is waiting for you to give you a calming, nurturing experience. It may not look like a spa, per se, but the therapist would tailor the experience to give you the same feeling.

The advisors are coaches and are able to deliver the therapy of trust and professionalism — someone with whom you discuss your personal issues, and who delivers a service that you cannot manage on your own without him or her.

Would there be a reception desk where you could check in, get comfortable and understand the "norm" about tipping, which is based on how satisfying your experience was? If you were treated with respect and dignity, and given some advice to act upon immediately, is it conceivable that a $20 or $25 tip is within the realm of normal? If you are not satisfied or if you feel you were not treated properly, no tip is necessary.

Referrals, of course, are actually a way of tipping. Maddock Douglas started working with our financial advisor more than 15 years ago. Over the years, we've referred dozens of people to him. We understand he makes money managing the company's 401(k) plan, but that wasn't enough. He deserved a tip—so we shared social currency and recommended him to others.

While the insurance world would have a hard time imagining that someone would actually pay more through tips for an experience that is seen as unpleasant, herein lies the opportunity. Make it pleasant. Make it amazing. Make it something that is far better than tolerable but downright word-of-mouth worthy.

Now, does everything have to evolve the way I just described it? Of course not. There could be hybrid models that bridge what I have been discussing and what currently exist. Or you might come up with ways to divide jobs differently. For example (and leave potential licensing requirements aside for the moment), we might start dividing up the work like they do in a physician's office. When you go to an ophthalmologist today, she is no longer doing the routine stuff like putting drops in your eyes or checking your current prescriptions. Various technicians are doing that. The doctor concentrates on examining your eyes, looking for potential signs of trouble.

We might have people whose sole job is to sell term insurance, if that turns out to be the right choice. And commissioned (and/or tipped) agents would sell the more complicated products.

The point is, imagine our industry if it was being invented today and did not exist before. How would you do things?

If you don't change our existing model, you can bet someone from the outside will.

What would American Express, H&R Block and Bank of America do? Leveraging the power of unfelt money

This idea is actually the sequel to the one before. In the last section, I talked about how people could get paid differently. In this case, we can look more at the tensions of consumers who don't want to pay for things that aren't seen as having immediate value to them.

"I would like to have insurance because it would help me to protect myself/my family if something should happen, but I can't fit it into my monthly expenses."

Because insurance is not a tangible benefit, consumers feel the premium payments are a major "pinch" to their budgets. But what about currencies that are not so pinchy? Specifically, I am talking about the concept of "unfelt money." Unfelt money is the income, cash, assets or other currencies that are generally not relied upon for monthly living expenses. Examples of unfelt money are/could be: rewards points from credit cards/airlines/retailers, tax refunds, birthday gifts, spot bonuses, security deposit refunds, small gambling winnings.

So how can we really make this work?

Suppose that individuals — particularly those who don't think they can afford much insurance, whether it be health, life, auto, home, etc. — funneled their "points," their spare change, their little windfalls, etc., into an insurance "fund." And then they paid whatever they could on top of it, perhaps $10 or $20 a week.

In exchange, they would be able to dip into that pool for "claims" at a benefit rate that was commensurate with the amount they paid – and the amount the pool is worth as converted to the risk. (More on this in a minute.)

If we were to play the WW____D game, contemplating what other financial institutions might do to solve this problem, the solutions might look like this:

American Express, à la its Membership Rewards program, would probably establish the point/exchange rate currency value at $1 equals one point and then price rewards (benefits/payouts in our case) accordingly.

H&R Block would figure out a way to make a tax refund payment (partly or fully) deposited directly into an insurance account. They do that now for their premier customers by letting them pay their preparation fees through their refund.

Bank of America would give the customer a credit card that rounds every purchase up to the next dollar and would take the difference (the purchase was for $63.27, but Bank of America charged you $64; the difference here being 73 cents) and put it into some kind of an insurance product.

You could value the points in a simple way: $1 might equal 100 points.

I have a hunch that younger consumers today do not really distinguish much between "types" of insurance. They just want to know their risks are covered. Actually, that is more than just a hunch, it is borne out in much of the research we have done around Gen Y and insurance. To them, there is a very blurry line between auto, health, home and life insurance.

So if that is the case, then don't bog them down with buying so many different kinds of policies. Just remember my discussion about "lifestyle continuity" (see Chapter 1) and define your product as one that makes sure their plans are not messed up. After all, that's what they care about.

So what might this kind of program look like? How about this:

Suggest that young people contribute $10 or $20 a week to a "risk" reward points account and then link that account to all their sources of unfelt income: points they received for credit card purchases, airline miles, etc.

At the end of a couple of years, at $100 a point, they could have 400,000 points accumulated in that time frame.

Then suppose there is a situation where a person has a "lifestyle continuity" issue. It could be anything…illness, car breakage, job loss, computer crash, illness of a relative, unplanned pregnancy, a flood in the basement…anything. She could then go to her risk-reward points account and redeem some points for cash or services. The value of the service would vary depending upon the same variables that go into pricing insurance.

(For illustration purposes only. I don't want any actuarial challenges or nitpicky pricing geek comments, or questions about assumptions or why I stopped at 400,000. Yes, I am talking to you, Mr. Smarty-pants.)

	50,000 – 100,000 Points	100,001 – 200,000 Points	200,001 – 400,000 Points	400,000+ Points
Job Loss	$100/week	$175/week	$350/week	$500/week
Short-term Illness (6 weeks)	$350/week	$425/week	$500/week	$750/week
Long-term Illness (12 weeks)	$150/week	$200/week	$300/week	$400/week
Car Breakage	$500	$650	$850	$1,000
Illness of Family Member	$1,000	$2,000	$3,000	$4,000
Property Loss	$750	$1,000	$1,250	$1,750
Divorce	$500	$750	$1,000	$1,300
Death	$10,000	$15,000	$25,000	$45,000
Cash, No Questions Asked	$500	$1,000	$2,000	$4,000

There would be no insurance applications to fill out (just a simple form to complete when you sign up for the program) and, of course, an iPhone app to manage all this once you did.

Hmmm, could this be the young person's insurance starter kit? Upgradeable to the real deal sometime in the future…for points? Cash? Social currency? **(More on social currency, next.)**

The whole idea of a starter kit is an interesting area to explore. From early childhood, we are taught to begin with a simple version of a product and upgrade as we get older, from crayons to Monte Blancs and tricycles to Harleys, people like the idea of simple to complex. We almost see it as a rite of passage. Are we training our folks to take advantage of this kind of behavior? Are we giving them the tools to do so? Or has term insurance become the tool of last resort?

What would Zipcar, Redbox and Occupy do? Leveraging the power of collaborative consumption and social movement

The term "collaborative consumption" is used to describe the rapid increase in sharing, swapping and repurposing of goods made possible by massive social connectivity. Why own a car or a DVD when you are only going to use it sometimes, or maybe only once.

Can we tap into that concept?

Zipcar, Redbox and even eBay (through its newly started rental program) have figured out collaborative consumption.

So what does this have to do with insurance? Well, at the risk of sounding biased, I would say the insurance industry invented collaborative consumption hundreds of years ago. That is not to say that people didn't share their goods and services at all before then, but I think we got there first — and did it better. Why own all of the financial risk of your own disability, property loss or death? Why not "collaborate" with people in your communities and states, pool your resources together, and create a "fund" that will pay out for those in need, when they need it? **Eureka! What a great idea!**

So the insight for insurance may have sounded like this:

"I would like to protect my family against financial risk because I don't want our future plans jeopardized, but I don't have enough money to set aside for big financial disasters."

The trouble is that, today, people do not see how we have solved for that need. Instead, they lament when they do not get their "money's worth." This has always been ironic to me because, in order to get your money's worth, you have to have something bad happen to you. Which would you rather have? Peace of mind? Or a serious problem? (...after which the insurance company tries to make you whole.)

What most of the public does not realize is that insurance is like "upside down" lotto. You buy a lotto ticket knowing you are unlikely to win, but you play because you might. Insurance works the exact same way, except that nobody likes the prize.

But most consumers really don't think about it this way. And it is our fault. We haven't done a very good job explaining how our industry works and how we make money. (See my discussion about Transparency in Chapter 9.)

The only consumers who have any chance of knowing how insurance works are the 2.3 million people who the Bureau of Labor Statistics says are employed by the industry. That's less than 1 percent of the population.

The other 99 percent have no clue. If they understood how companies price their products, and how the public's good or bad habits impact rates, perhaps they would behave differently. If we put in big, bold print **"BECAUSE YOU ARE A SMOKER, YOU ARE PAYING 18 PERCENT MORE A YEAR THAN YOU HAVE TO,"** would behavior change?

And if we communicated that the reckless behavior of the few—and we could single out people who speed excessively or drive without insurance—are raising the rates of everyone else, would it cause responsible people to put social pressure on those who are not?

Is it time for a movement around being a responsible insured?

That may sound far-fetched, but social acceptance is the only way a movement can be successful. Insurance companies cannot expect that they can teach this lesson to the public alone, simply by raising rates, rejecting applications or litigating. It requires peer pressure.

Think back. I can remember a time in the early '70s when it was socially acceptable to throw trash out your car window while driving. Not anymore.

I can remember a time in the '80s and '90s when people didn't actively take each other's car keys when they had too much to drink, or weren't aware of the implications of second-hand smoke. Not anymore. I can remember times not so many years ago when nobody would look at you crooked for throwing plastic bottles and aluminum cans in the regular trash. Not anymore.

Decade	Social awareness of...
1970s	Littering
1980s	Smoking/Second-hand Smoke
1990s	Drinking and Driving
2000s	Protecting the Environment
2010s?	Responsible Insurance Behavior?

What do all these things have in common? It's changing behavior for the greater good. The acts of the few can impact the many. Isn't that how insurance works?

Maybe it is time for a movement in this decade to make it socially unacceptable to be an irresponsible insured.

Who will lead that charge? One company? A group of companies? An association? Or someone else who has the public's ear?

Could this be the next Occupy? There is enough angst about the industry to get people fired up. Why not channel it effectively?

What would (did) LearnVest do? A Napster moment in the making for financial services?

We may have a Napster moment in the making as you read this.

Online financial education and advice startup firm LearnVest has not only raised $25 million in venture capital, but it just launched a series of prepackaged, e-enabled financial plans that are accessible to the masses and priced between $69 and $349. (www.learnvest.com)

For many years, financial services firms have either been trying to figure out how to reach the masses efficiently — OR avoid them completely — focusing on the affluent and wealthy markets. After all, like Willie Sutton said, "That's where the money is."

While the rest of the financial services world is waiting for the younger, less affluent people to inherit the money of their boomer parents, LearnVest found a different opportunity — **a currently unmet need**. The need is to understand and act on a plan that will help those with little or no money to get out of debt, create wealth and manage it well; the need to trust the people with whom they are dealing; the need to ask professionals instead of their parents, coworkers or siblings for guidance.

And the insight is:

"I would like to have a financial plan because it will help me have the future I want, but I am not sure I have enough money for an advisor to care about me."

Not only does solving for this need mean trouble for our industry, but Suze Orman should watch her back too. For many years, she and a few others, like Dave Ramsey, had the model that was the only game in town for the people unserved by the financial advisors. That model is a mashup of opinion, entertainment and generally "unidirectional" dialogue that results in the sale of books, videos and tickets to seminars. Suze doesn't really make her income from designing her audience's outcome. Granted, she has helped many people start to get out of debt with her advice. The trouble is, she just doesn't know who they are. More important, what do they do next?

Most of them can't turn to "real" financial advisors who offer the plan, the guidance and the products to go with it. They are busy figuring out how to improve their income by continually moving up market, targeting people with the most money.

And that leaves a huge opportunity for the LearnVests and Mint.coms of the world.

The reaction in our industry to that statement is as predictable as the sunrise. When asked about these fledgling companies, senior executives say things like:

1. That can't possibly be profitable if the advice is any good (**cynicism**)
2. That's not the way to deliver financial advice; it has to be face to face (**sticking to what used to work**)
3. We'll just see how good they are (**sidelining**)

If you find yourself making statements like this, consider the notion that these kinds of statements are the three deadly signs of leaders in an industry that is facing its Napster moment.

Innovators would ask questions about what LearnVest is doing. Questions are so much more powerful than statements because they open up possibility and curiosity — and keep you in a perpetual state of wonder.

So the questions that the innovators in the industry might ask are:

1. What was their insight?
2. How are they making it profitable?
3. Will these innovations spill over into the more affluent market?
4. What will they do next?
5. What should I be doing to capitalize or even improve upon their offering?

If you find yourself asking these questions and maybe others — awesome. It means you are in the right mindset for staying ahead — and capitalizing on opportunities that fill a real need in the market.

If you find yourself making statements about why companies like LearnVest will never succeed — beware.

WWYD? (Monday morning, that is)

The Napster moment section of this book is intended to inspire thought and, more important, action on the part of someone who wants to make a difference in an industry that is very important but suffering from a lack of innovation.

Out of 100 people with whom we meet in the industries that Maddock Douglas works, maybe five are truly ready, willing and able to make significant change that reinvents their business for the better. While it may sound like we are trying to get that number higher, we're not. We're just looking for them — and trying to get them inspired enough to act on their innovation intentions and abilities because 5 percent is all it really takes to make a difference.

So **W**hat **W**ould **Y**ou **D**o Monday morning if you are one of the 5 percent?

1. **Respect the past.** Spend some time studying the origins of insurance as a social construct.

2. **Be curious.** Visit some newer models in services of all kinds. Check out State Farm's "Next Door" model in Chicago.
   http://chicagobrander.com/2011/07/11/state-farm-becoming-a-better-neighbor-with-next-door-concept/
   Visit a Massage Envy. Look at how companies have redefined what it means to be in a certain business. (The classic example: Starbucks redefining the coffee shop.)

3. **Find parallels.** Examine entities that are emerging that help people in need. Give Forward is a good one. It is a for-profit company that uses the power of the Web to raise money for people who don't have insurance.

4. **Recognize breakthroughs.** Check out LearnVest.com. Look at how they communicate and what they offer.

5. **Come up with your own set of potential Napster moments.** Can you list five ways your business could be reinvented?

6. **Inspire others to come along with you.** Take these ideas to your next staff meeting, or to a meeting with your peers.

7. **Follow a proven process.** Don't try to shoot from the hip; do what you know works well. Read *Brand New: Solving the Innovation Paradox* for help.

8. **Be grateful.** Grateful people look for possibility and expect to find it. They look for the treasure in everything they encounter. They look for the reasons to move ahead versus stay behind. We are grateful you have read this book and given us a chance to help you change your own course, your industry and the world.

Thank you!